In a world that gets its news through sound bites, finds its closest friends through social media, and gets its worth through how it's perceived by others, it is easy to approach a relationship with Jesus through a superficial, shallow lens.

Rooting us in the narrative of scripture, Evan Oxner points us toward a Jesus that doesn't want to simply make an appearance in our lives, giving us an "airbrushed" appearance to the world around us, but brings us a Gospel that changes us and transforms all aspects of our lives.

In *Let's Be Blunt,* Evan points us toward a Jesus worth following and one that wants to help us experience the new life He came to offer us—life that can make a real difference to those in our world that we are in a position to influence. I highly recommend that we read, reflect on, and discern the message of this book, allowing it to influence what it means to be a follower of Christ.

—Rob McDowell
Pastor & Leadership Coach, Divine Renovations

Let's Be Blunt is not written for timid people seeking easy answers. Evan Oxner wrestles with hard questions and invites you to join him in relentlessly pursuing truth. Be prepared. He doesn't settle for cliché responses, and you may not always agree with his conclusions. But don't be surprised if you come away with fresh insights and stronger faith.

—Mark Gorveatte
Crossroads District Superintendent, Wesleyan Church
Author of *Lead Like Wesley*

If you were to combine the brazen bluntness of the Apostle Peter with a hint of C.S. Lewis and Gregory Boyd, you might come up with something similar to this. Evan Oxner isn't worried about ruffling feathers and kicking up dirt as he journeys through the grand narrative of Scripture, prodding you to evaluate the accuracy of your current picture of the Gospel.

—Joel Gorveatte
Lead Pastor, Moncton Wesleyan Church

I am a thirty-four-year-old woman raised in the Church who has a strong faith and continues to question many aspects of the Church, while working in a field that deals every day with the brokenness of the world. This book asks the questions and puts into words what we all are—or should be—thinking. It shows the truth of Jesus beneath everything else we have brought into it, and shows the beautiful simplicity of what the life and death of Jesus has given us. For those questioning, or comfortable in, or outside of faith: you should read this book.

—Mary B.
Professional

Evan is a straight shooter with a passionate heart for God's purpose. He writes with intensity and refuses to avoid the hard questions. I am confident his perspective will help many in their faith journey.

—Dr. L.D. Buckingham
CEO, Buckingham Leadership Institute

The writing of this young author is thought-provoking, reflecting a fresh approach to an ancient topic. *Let's Be Blunt*—I commend this book to you.

—H.C. Wilson
General Superintendent Emeritus, Wesleyan Church

Oxner's book begins with an explosive retelling of a familiar story and continues as an accessible and clear reminder of who we are as the Church. Writing with a pastor's heart, he reminds us to be uncomfortable and amazed with God and life once again. We are reminded that God has a personality and desires a two-way relationship with us, and that *where* we spend eternity is not as important as *how* we spend eternity.

Oxner calls us to remember that there is more to the Christian life, and that it shouldn't be like "wandering around an airport checking out all the rare goodies at restaurants and souvenir shops while waiting to leave. There everything is overpriced and will most likely be confiscated by security or customs." There is more.

In an increasingly polarized world, it is refreshing to read a pastoral and thoughtful call to a part of the Kingdom and Gospel which is intended to affect everything in both profound and simple ways. A worthwhile and meaningful read!

—Rev. J. Sheldon MacLeod
Regional Director, Atlantic Canada
Evangelical Fellowship of Canada

LET'S BE
BLUNT

What's Really the Point of Christianity?

EVAN OXNER

LET'S BE BLUNT
Copyright © 2020 by Evan Oxner

Quotations by C.S. Lewis used by permission:
The Problem of Pain © copyright CS Lewis Pte Ltd 1940.
Till We Have Faces © copyright CS Lewis Pte Ltd 1956.

Scripture quotations marked ESV are from the ESV® Bible (The Holy Bible, English Standard Version®). Copyright © 2001 by Crossway Bibles, a publishing ministry of Good News Publishers. Used by permission. All rights reserved. Scripture quotations marked MSG are from THE MESSAGE. Copyright© 1993, 1994, 1995, 1996, 200, 2001, 2002. Used by permission of NavPress Publishing Group. Scripture quotations marked NIV are from The Holy Bible, New International Version® NIV® Copyright © 1973, 1978, 1984, 2011 by Biblica, Inc.TM Used by permission. All rights reserved worldwide. Scripture quotations marked NLT are taken from the Holy Bible, New Living Translation Copyright © 1996, 2004, 2015 by Tyndale House Foundation. Used by permission of Tyndale House Publishers, Inc., Carol Stream, Illinois 60188. All rights reserved.

Printed in Canada

Print ISBN: 978-1-4866-1950-4
eBook ISBN: 978-1-4866-1951-1

Word Alive Press
119 De Baets Street, Winnipeg, MB R2J 3R9
www.wordalivepress.ca

Cataloguing in Publication may be obtained through Library and Archives Canada

CONTENTS

The command we have from Christ is blunt: Loving God includes loving people. You've got to love both.

—1 John 4:21, MSG

And we all, who with unveiled faces contemplate the Lord's glory, are being transformed into his image with ever-increasing glory, which comes from the Lord, who is the Spirit.

—2 Corinthians 3:18, NIV

Special thanks to the Newsboys for their song "Lost the Plot."
You set the stage for this book.[1]

CHAPTER ONE

THE EXODUS

"Get out! *Get out now!*" His voice boomed and echoed through the halls with fury and bile.

Standing, he prepared another volley.

"You come in here with your pretentious outlook, your tricks and your demands. You are so smug! You come and tell me what to do, tell me what to change, tell me what I can and cannot do in my own country."

Turning, he grabbed his sword and pointed it straight at his guest.

"You terrorize my people, you ruin my resources, you insult me by your very presence, and even try to tell me what I should be doing with my own people!"

Growing silent, something began to change in his face. The rage shifted—he was no longer a man who had been challenged, but one who had been violated. To glance into his eyes but for a second would have driven his every emotion into your own soul. The silence hung in the air for only a short moment before he spoke again.

"And after all this, you have even somehow managed to enter the homes of my citizens—even my own home—and have murdered our innocents.

"My son is dead because of you!"

Every muscle in his body quaked.

"And how and why and…" he spat, "you don't even talk, you just have your friend here do the talking for you! I hate you… *I hate you!"*

He sat down, defeated and exhausted. Tossing his sword on the ground, he said, "Take your people. Get out of my land. I never want to see you or your cursed race again. Just get out!"

His words were sharp. This was all that could be said. This was all that would be said.

This was their cue. Moses and Aaron turned around and walked out of Pharaoh's palace. The Israelites were finally free from their slavery; they could now return to the land God had promised them. After all the years of pain and suffering, after all their trials and problems, they were finally free.

As I have studied the Bible, and delved into the life of man and God, I have come across some really crazy things. Things that I did not expect. Things I was not sure I believed. I have spent a lot of time in my short life wrestling with all of these things, and I am sure that there will be many more restless nights as I continue my attempt to understand creation. But, with all of my theories and limitless questions, I believe there is a single truth from which we must all begin if we are to figure anything out. It is a truth that is stated in the book of Genesis, and seen before that in the events of the Exodus.

Yes, you read that correctly. This truth was seen before what was explicitly stated in the book of Genesis. I am not attempting to reorder the books of the Bible, or to skew any historical or theological chronology. All I want to point out in this observation is that when God gave Moses the Pentateuch (the first five books of the Bible as we have it), in whatever way He did, Moses and the

Israelites would have already known and personally experienced the events of their Exodus.

Genesis would have been a later experience for the people, or at least a more distant and separate experience. They were freed from slavery in the Exodus, and then later received the revelation of Genesis. Thus, the Exodus would have been the original encounter with this truth, and because of that I wish to begin this theology and all other aspects of truth, value, direction, and meaning from what the Exodus reveals.

This is where we start.

And I have to warn you upfront, this is not a pleasant revelation. I think it is valuable, and when we come to terms with it, it becomes the driving force of our very existence, but it is not an enjoyable process.

The story of the Exodus systematically deconstructs every insufficient thing we depend on. It reveals every point of foundation that won't hold. It breaks apart every safeguard and argument that we have used to fight our battles, but won't stand the test of time.

The people, habits, routines, financial plans, relationships, social norms, and religious assumptions that we have held onto, hoping against reality they will keep us safe, get exposed for what they are: false gods. Anything we depend on that can't actually provide what we need is a false god or idol.

But once we get rid of them, what we are left with isn't simply our starting point, but a foundation that will last, won't fall apart, and can actually provide what we need. We are left with a God that can actually deliver.

At the time of the Exodus, the Israelites had been in slavery for hundreds of years, but had grown in number so greatly that Pharaoh was committing infanticide in order to control the population and maintain his dominance. When we read the book of Exodus, we see that out of this horrific crime comes the desperate attempt of a young woman to save her newborn son. Her son's name was Moses, and through a series of quite remarkable and unpredictable events, he ended up being raised in the palace of Pharaoh by his own mother. When Moses became an adult, he decided to stand against the injustice he saw and ended up killing an Egyptian who was beating an Israelite. Then, as is the common response for most men, Moses refused to face the consequences of his actions, began to doubt who he was, and ran away.

After being away from Egypt for forty years, Moses eventually received a call from God to deliver the Israelites out of slavery and bring them to the home that Abraham (their ancestor) had founded and established for them. Though it has been related ad nauseam, most people either consider this event to be some sort of outrageous children's story or simply don't think about it at all, but this is an event to which we need to pay very close attention. This is where we see God speaking to Moses from a bush that was on fire, but not burning. But the bush isn't the important part. What's important is who started the conversation.

It was God.

God began the process. God initiated the conversation. God called first. Remember this.

God called Moses to go back to Egypt to free the Israelites from slavery.

Then Moses asked an important question: "Who exactly am I supposed to tell them has sent me? Who are you, and why should we listen?"

The answer to that question is essential to everything that will be discussed in this book.

In Exodus 3:14, we find God's response. God tells Moses to say to the people, *"I AM has sent me to you"* (NIV).

At first glance, this seems like a rather vague answer—almost as if God is attempting to avoid the question—but in reality, the only reason we think it vague is because everything else must be defined through comparison. There is nothing we know through experience that has its definition solely as *being*. And yet, there it is. This statement is linked to the Hebrew name for God, "YHWH" (there are no vowels in the original Hebrew), pronounced "Yah-Weh" and meaning "I AM WHO I AM."

God isn't of this world. This world was created; He was not. That's why the only name that can be used to accurately describe Him is one that uses Himself as the definition. There is nothing in this world, or the rest of the universe, that would do to describe or define God besides Himself. No comparison will do. He is who He is. *He is the definition. He* is the source. *He* is the beginning and the end. *He* is.

All that *is* is based in Him. Nothing is without Him. This is not to say that everything is part of God, or God is part of everything. Created things are completely separate in what they are, but their design, the physical nature and law that keep time and space functioning, are because of God. Creation, the universe, is based on the qualities and dynamics of His nature, His work, and His being, which reflect Himself.

I believe Moses had much the same reaction that we do when first hearing God's response. I think he was confused, skeptical, and maybe a bit frustrated. But Moses went back to Egypt anyway, and God sent Moses' brother Aaron along with him to do the talking.

Once they got to Egypt, they went to Pharaoh and they began the negotiations. And by "negotiations," I mean the demands and arguments. Pharaoh didn't want to lose his workforce, and God wouldn't let Moses take "no" for an answer.

This is where the deconstruction begins.

When Pharaoh refused to release the Israelites from slavery, God got to work. Each step in His plan signified, and actually enacted, God's dominance.

The Egyptians depended on Ra, the god of the sun. So YHWH made the sky go dark, except where He wanted there to be light. Ra was unable to stop Him, to slow Him down, or to deliver in any way. Ra couldn't give the Egyptians what they needed.

The Egyptians depended on the Nile, which provided water for seventy percent of the population. It was their source of life.

So God turned it into blood. He turned their source of life into a sign of death to show that the Nile couldn't deliver—it couldn't give life; it couldn't provide what they needed.

Most people lived near the Nile because it was one of the very few places anything would grow; so, to prove another point, God wiped out the crops.

Egyptians believed in a god that looked like a frog (believed to be the god of fertility). They worshipped this god in their obsession with sex and abundance. So God sent a plague of frogs—so many that they couldn't be contained. Their worship of this "god" backfired.

Ra and the Nile were nothing but false gods.

Crops and agriculture turned out to be false gods.

Fertility, sex, even family were revealed to be just false gods.

And God continued to tear down their world. But despite sign after sign, argument after argument, Pharaoh refused to let the Israelites go. The only god left to be challenged—to be dethroned, torn down—was Pharaoh himself.

Humanity idolizes itself above all other things, and that is made most obvious in how desperately we hold to our pride. It was in challenge to this pride that God sent an angel of death to kill the firstborn in every home that did not submit to Him. This event is called the Passover because the angel passed-over any home that obeyed God, leaving them safe and sound. In this act, Pharaoh's own son was killed, revealing that even he and his family could not last.

It was evident Yahweh was greater than all of these "gods."

These gods may seem ancient and irrelevant, but they are not unlike the gods we depend on today. Imagine God tearing down all the things that we put our trust in.

- Our cars would break down at the worst possible moment
- Our vacation plans would be ruined by flight delays, illness, and bad weather

- Our favourite shows would get cancelled
- We would convert everything to green energy sources, and still the climate would change
- We would have enormous amounts of money in our bank accounts, and still feel empty
- The grocery store would close the minute we arrived in a rush
- Alarm clocks would fail to go off
- Each person would find the love of their life, but they'd still be drawn to others, to porn, to work, or just be faced with disappointment
- The internet would provide nothing but false information
- Cell service would go down
- The news would report every couple of months on how our food is killing us
- The weather forecast would never be predictably right or wrong
- Cancer treatments would only delay death, not stop it
- Pride and arrogance would successfully keep us safe from others, but tear us down from the inside out
- We would bet on people, and be consistently betrayed by their selfishness

Hmm, perhaps those things we depend on can't deliver either. Perhaps we have been trusting in false gods. Perhaps everything we have based our lives on can't really give us what we need.

Looking at that list, I'm thinking to myself, "I don't depend on those things!" But I know how upset I get, how frustrated I feel, how hopeless, stressed, anxious, and angry I am when those things happen. I wouldn't have those reactions if I wasn't so dependent on them, if they weren't my false gods.

So here we are, back where we started.

After the plagues left their mark on Pharaoh, he finally allowed the Israelites to leave. But Pharaoh never wanted to do the right thing. He just wanted the threat to stop, and God knew his heart, so He decided to make an example out of him. After the Israelites packed up and left, they eventually reached what seemed to be an impassible barrier, the Red Sea, and Pharaoh assembled his army to come after them. His gods may have been conquered and shown to be useless, but he still had his own army, his own strength, his own life—and he would use it to take back what he felt was rightfully his.

Standing at the edge of the Red Sea, taking in the situation around them, the Israelites began to panic. In front of them was this giant body of water, too deep and wide for an entire nation to swim across with their families, possessions, and livestock. Behind them were Pharaoh and his army, determined to either force them back into slavery or destroy them. On either side of them were hills and pagan people, groups who opposed God and His ways, and whom God would later call the Israelites to get rid of. They were literally surrounded by physical, social, and spiritual boundaries. Every option was hostile and impossible.

When people are cornered, they do stupid things, and the Israelites were no different. Their panic overwhelmed them, and they started making plans of how they were going to give in and surrender to Pharaoh. After all that God had done, they found themselves in yet another troubling situation and instantly forgot who God was and what He was capable of. They saw the strength of nature, the popularity of paganism, and the power of man, and forgot about God. After all the signs and wonders, they still didn't believe God was who He said He was; they still thought that a man with an army could defeat Him if the circumstances were right. The people had actually become so panicked and desperate that they started to think that Moses had brought them out of Egypt just to be killed.

This may be the most important passage in the entire Bible, and as we go through this book, I hope you will see why. It was here that God, after tearing down the false gods, made it clear who He is.

God saw all this happening and told Moses to say to the people:

The Lord himself will fight for you. Just stay calm.
—Exodus 14:14, NLT

God will fight the battle for you. And you? You keep your mouths shut!
—Exodus 14:14, MSG

I prefer The Message translation of this verse, because it expresses so well the meaning and emotion behind the words used in this passage. The word for "just stay calm" or "hold your peace" or "keep your mouths shut" in the original Hebrew is *charash*, and it can be translated in a variety of ways, but they all have this kind of forced and potent feeling behind them, as if the nature of the word is a blunt, harsh or necessary demand.[2] When looking at the ways *charash* can be translated, it is apparent that God wasn't just asking the Israelites to give Him some time and be patient with Him, if they were willing to allow that. It is clear that God was bellowing down from Heaven a command that *must* be followed. Either sit down and shut up, or be killed by Pharaoh. Those were the options. *Charash!* Sit down, zip your lips, and watch *God* work!

God then told Moses to stretch out his staff and part the sea. When Moses did this, wind blew in and parted the waters, making a dry path across the sea, and walls of water formed on either side of the path. The Israelites crossed over to the other side, and once they were safely there, God allowed Pharaoh to come after them. Like a sucker, Pharaoh took the bait, and once he and his army were in the middle of the sea, God stopped the winds and released the water, and Pharaoh and his army were engulfed in the weight of the sea.

In a single act, the most powerful leader of the most powerful nation with the most powerful army in the ancient world was defeated. The Israelites were saved, and Pharaoh was no more.

A single dominating thought was presented to the world in this event: the simple truth that God alone is God, and no one else can ever challenge Him. God will fight the battle. No one else will, and no one else can. The pagan gods won't fight for us, and they can't. Men won't fight for us, and if they do, they will not win. Nature and this broken world won't fight for us. When we try to fight for ourselves, we will find we are just as powerless as Pharaoh.

No, God is the only one who will fight for us, and we need to accept that. We need to understand that and act on that. We need to sit down and stop whining, complaining, fighting, struggling, and trying to find our own solutions. We need to sit down and shut up, because God will fight for us, and no one can stand against Him. He wants to fight for us—and He is the only one able to fight for us and win. Our false gods can't deliver.

God is the beginning and the end. There is nothing before Him and there is nothing after Him. All we are and everything we do takes its essential raw form and source from Him. This is where the Old Testament begins: *In the beginning God...* (Genesis 1:1, NIV).

If we are ever to understand the uniqueness, the power, the significance, or the usefulness of the basic reality of this universe, our existence, and this thing called the Gospel, we must begin with this simple point: God is YHWH... "I AM WHO I AM." If we were to start anywhere else, we would find that the compass is not pointed north, our northern star is skewed, and our sun rises and sets in some other direction than East and West.

This is not solely some kind of philosophical or religious perspective or conversation; this concerns ontology, epistemology, physics, anthropology, sociology, psychology, biology, and everything else. The very fabric of this world must begin with God. We can no longer depend on our false gods. Our perspectives and understanding must begin with YHWH, even when the world disagrees.

Our modern and postmodern understanding of the world is nothing new; it has been perpetuated throughout history by different means and different cultures and stories. It has been around since the time of the ancient Egyptians, or even back as far as the tower of Babel. It continued to the Roman Empire, to the Renaissance and René Descartes, to modern day ecumenicism and atheism. We have tried to put man at the centre of the universe and find unique ways to become worshippers either of the world, the self, or mankind in general. We continue to begin our ideas with man and end them with men, finding the same result in each generation.

René Descartes put a philosophy to this thought, and began the greatest downward spiral we have seen in recent history, a spiral that continues today. Descartes sought to develop a philosophy that was self-verifiable. In his philosophy, Descartes based everything on a controllable and provable idea—everything was limited to that which we can fully understand, and so was limited to our own creativity. Though this might make great science, humanity has never been able to create anything greater than itself; the creation never exceeds the creator. When we have based the universe on that which we can fully grasp, we have limited the universe to that which we could only understand and create, thus removing the transcendent.

Descartes made "self" the starting point. And though he later attempted to prove God's existence from this point, God remained limited by the mind and understanding of man, rather than vice versa. We made ourselves the foundation, the thing we depend on. We replaced the God who is the "I AM" with the statement, "I think, therefore I am." It is startling to see the similarity and blasphemy of the shift.

The contrast between modern theology/philosophy and true Biblical reality is the positioning of the initial being: who was "I am," and why? For Descartes, we were the first "am," because we think. For Israel, it was clear that God was the first "AM" simply because "I AM" or *He is.*

If we put man at the beginning and make him the centre, we get something less than reality and less than what we were designed for. This will always result in an existence that is incomplete and destined for corruption. Like the Israelites in Egypt, who were required to make bricks without the necessary materials, so too do we build and create a nice-looking brick that will eventually just fall apart, no matter how well we make it or how long we spend on it. Without the complete picture and necessary components, the work will only result in failure—and, inevitably, destruction.

The Church has fallen for the same kind of false information and ideology that Descartes did. Instead of putting God at the beginning, we have found that it is easier to put business, leadership, worship, popularity, humanitarian projects, people, numbers, money, gimmicks, tricks, needs, and ideas ahead of God. These have become our false gods.

Now, you may be looking at the page and thinking, "Well, aren't you are on a high horse. Not every church is like that." You may be right. Actually, you are right. There are some incredible churches doing some incredible things in North America and around the world. Yet, even though I can't pretend to know what every church is doing, I also can't pretend to ignore the staunch reality that the power that much of the current Church has is not the same power that was displayed in the Exodus... at least not the power displayed by our God. Perhaps it's the power displayed by Pharaoh, but not the power of God.

We depend on marketing campaigns, current trends, and worship music. We curb the gospel message so it isn't offensive, so it's easy for people to accept and join in without demanding much of them. We have perverted our message to the point that it must fall in line with certain good principles of leadership, business ethics, and culture, rather than allowing God to define that culture. We start with an idea and go from there, just as Descartes did.

Whether you believe the Bible or not, whether you believe what I have written here or not, this is my starting point. As you continue reading through this book, I believe you will see why it is essential that it must be *the* starting point.

We must begin here:

YHWH.

CHAPTER TWO

NO NONSENSE

This is your last chance. After this, there is no turning back. You take the blue pill, your story ends, you wake up in your bed and believe whatever you want to believe. You take the red pill, you stay in wonderland and I show you how deep the rabbit hole goes.

—Morpheus, *The Matrix*[3]

The vast majority of people in our day and age aren't used to straight and blunt honesty upon a first encounter. It is customary to begin every conversation with the cliché, and often completely false, exchange of,

"How are you today?"

"Good, how are you?"

Both are incredible displays of the current cultural norm of lying in everyday circumstances. Most people don't actually care how someone else is (as displayed by the awkward silence which follows a response other than "good"); further, most people aren't "good," but simply say so out of etiquette or the attempt to avoid any further prying questions.

Every day, we begin our interactions with a considerable portion of cow-manure, and we are well trained in the art of "cutting conversations short." And I mean that: it is an art. Learning how to talk our way out of a conversation, work a room, or point out some social issue in order to deflect the topic of discussion away from any personal or uncomfortable area of thought is an art. We sugarcoat (quite ironically) our interactions with nonsense in order to make the situation more relaxed and comfortable, continuing the façade that everything is fine, all in the hopes that by throwing on sufficient fertilizer we may find that our apple-pie dreams of utopian conversation may begin sprouting some manner of escape from the reality that haunts us. However, when this common practice is interrupted, everyone assumes some new game has begun, or some personal vendetta is being played out, whereby whatever honesty may be displayed is understood as some kind of a fight for dominance, or an attempt to sell oneself as something one really isn't.

We have entered into a state of normalcy in which even sincere honesty can be understood as just another lie.

There is one major flaw with this little dynamic of society and culture: The Matrix is not real.

In 1999, the Wachowski brothers produced a film based upon the basic philosophical principles of George Berkeley. The philosophy ponders the question of what reality is. Is reality something real outside of ourselves, or is it just an idea inside our own heads, a projection of what we alone feel and think? In the film, all humans have been enslaved by the machines humanity created, and have now been hooked up to power generators so that their biological heat and electrical conduction can be harvested to power the machines. But in order to sustain this power, the humans must remain alive, and so must be conscious at some level. Thus, the machines created an alternate state of reality to which all humans were connected through an implant in their brains. They would only ever think that this alternate reality was their real lives, and would live their whole lives in what was called the

Matrix. They could love, grow, have families, make money, eat steak, fight, build, cry, and even die in the Matrix, but for some people that wasn't good enough. Most people were completely unaware of the existence of the Matrix and just assumed it was reality, but some people discovered what had actually happened. Those few people managed to escape from the Matrix and were working to save others from it as well.

In this story, a man named Morpheus is looking for one particular person called Neo to free from the Matrix. When Morpheus finally finds him, Neo is given two pills, one blue and one red. If he takes the blue pill, everything will go back to the way it was, but if he takes the red pill, he will have his eyes opened to a whole new world.

When we live our entire lives in one reality and we are suddenly confronted with the idea that it's all a lie, we may not want to leave. And, seriously, why would we want to? Why would we want to leave our comfortable and happy life that's full of sunshine and opportunities just to enter a world that has been ravaged by war, is blackened by perpetual clouds, is populated by machines, and where the human race has been reduced to biological batteries? (This may not be so different from our world as it is today.)

Because... whether they like it or not, whether they believe it or not, that is the reality of the situation, and outside of the truth, nothing actually changes or has value. There it is. The red pill. The thing that we must confront next along the journey of this book...

Outside of the truth, nothing has value.

We can imagine, play, dream, pretend, lie, and form our own creative reality, but in the end those things will fade into nothing—because they *are* nothing. Pretending we have money doesn't give us money. People throughout North America function as if it does—and despite all the credit cards (plastic that provides imaginary money) and long-term payment methods, the debt collectors still call, bankruptcy still happens, and the people with the money still end up shutting everyone else down.

Pretending we have friends doesn't actually mean we aren't lonely. Facebook, social media, following celebrities so closely that we know intimate details about their lives as *if* we knew them (the basis of the entire pop-culture environment and market), sharing our ideas whether they are worth sharing or not, getting the laughs at the parties and having lots of people know our name, will still result in no one actually knowing us. We will still know—deep down, below all the calluses, the baggage, and the lies—that we are still alone.

But what if that wasn't true? What if we could fool ourselves so well that we didn't even realize that the world we were living in wasn't real? What if we actually thought it was reality, and we were completely content and fulfilled living in it?

Maybe all we really need is the *experience* of it. Actually, one of the characters in *The Matrix* who had been set free to live in the real world decided that's what he wanted. He wanted to go back into the Matrix because the experience was worth it to him. For him, the lie was better than the truth.

There are a good many people in this world who feel the same way. When they are confronted with the truth, they will deny it and avoid it. They will dodge it, put up walls, avoid conversations, buy more distractions, and fill their lives with things to create such an elaborate lie that they don't have time to question it.

Lies might be easier to swallow.

Stories may be simpler to live with.

But we know they fall short, even as we go through them.

And we know that when it comes to the end, we will face the reality...

Sin hurts

Death sucks

Smoking kills

Cancer invades

Money never lasts

Happiness isn't bought

People die

Love is worth it
The best things are the things we need to fight for
Only God is God
And...
The truth shall set us free.

We may want to continue the façade. We may not want to live with the truth—and that is our choice—but we will always know something is missing, and in the end everything we had and did will be shown to be absolutely worthless. We will get to the end of our lives, and despite all the pleasures and memories we have accumulated, we will be haunted by the lack of purpose and meaning. We will find that nothing we had or did had any lasting value, and even though the experiences were incredible, they were just lies.

I hate being lied to.

I *hate* it.

If there is one thing you can do to push my buttons, it is to lie to me.

Lies are not real.

And if we are going to deal with anything of value, we need to deal only with what is real.

This is absolutely vital to what comes next, for without the truth, any attempt to change anything would simply be a matter of drawing designs in the air with a sparkler. The designs will fade the moment the instrument has passed. We need to know where we really are, who we really are, what we are really doing, and where we really need to go. As long as we are tolerating any level of nonsense in any area of our lives, we will be stuck in limbo, attempting to live in a world that doesn't actually exist.

Changing the world in our imaginations doesn't change the world in reality. Fixing our marriages by putting on a good show will not save our families. Dealing with our addictions (and it doesn't matter what they are) by fooling ourselves and others that everything is under control will never actually bring sanity or serenity, and will never rid us of the power they hold over us. When we go home, they will still be there. Growing relationships based upon social norms of shallow exchanges and obnoxious gestures of insincerity will never render a heart that actually cares about people, nor will it facilitate an environment where people learn that they are loved for who they are—inside and out, regardless of present circumstances. Faking the answers to deep questions and thoughts won't propel us deeper into the heart of God; it will only build another wall keeping us from it.

Now, I think this is where we get to the real hard part. No nonsense means no walls. It means, we're going to have to trust someone else to guard us. Because to be real means to be honest, and to be honest means to be vulnerable. And no one likes feeling vulnerable—we like feeling safe. We like being safe. So we need someone to protect us and keep us safe, because our lies will not protect us nor give us freedom.

There is only one who can keep us safe, and that is God. Only God will fight for us, and only He will set us free, because He is the great I AM. He is the truth. This is what John wrote about Jesus:

> So Jesus said to the Jews who had believed him, "If you abide in my word, you are truly my disciples, and you will know the truth, and the truth will set you free." They answered him, "We are offspring of Abraham and have never been enslaved to anyone. How is it that you say, 'You will become free'?"
>
> Jesus answered them, "Truly, truly, I say to you, everyone who practices sin is a slave to sin. The slave does not remain in the house forever; the son remains forever. So if the Son sets you free, you will be free indeed. I know that you are offspring of Abraham; yet you seek to kill me because my word finds no place in you. I speak of what I have seen with my Father, and you do what you have heard from your father."
>
> —John 8:31–38, ESV

*Thomas said to him, "Lord, we do not know where you are
going. How can we know the way?" Jesus said to him, "I
am the way, and the truth, and the life. No one comes to
the Father except through me. If you had known me, you
would have known my Father also. From now on you do
know him and have seen him."*

*Philip said to him, "Lord, show us the Father, and it
is enough for us." Jesus said to him, "Have I been with you
so long, and you still do not know me, Philip? Whoever
has seen me has seen the Father. How can you say, 'Show
us the Father'? Do you not believe that I am in the Father
and the Father is in me? The words that I say to you I do
not speak on my own authority, but the Father who dwells
in me does his works."*

—John 14:5–10, ESV

Now hold up: many of us have read those passages hundreds
of times, but I want us to take another slow look at them before we
read the rest of this chapter (there isn't much left). Look at them.
The parts that usually stick out to us aren't what I want us to see.

Do you see the connection between the truth and the being
of God?

Do you see how what the Exodus showed is amplified in this
statement of Christ?

Do you see the unity of the Father and the Son?

Do you see the illusions that these people believed before
Jesus opened their eyes?

Do you see how even in Jesus' work it always comes back
to God?

Do you see the unity between God and the truth, and how
He must be the definition if we are to find value... or freedom?

We are now back where we should be, everything starting
with God. The illusion of freedom is simply blind slavery. It has
no value. Our walls, games, masks, lies, and deceptions are but
an illusion created to allow someone else to control and use us

to power their own will. If we want to continue being slaves, by all means we can continue to live in the Matrix—but as for me, I choose to have the fulfillment that comes from knowing a reality that starts with what makes reality real: the truth. Without Christ, without the Truth, without God, we are slaves, and we are being manipulated to be something we weren't meant to be, and probably don't really want to be. So, if we want a life that is valuable, we must begin it with God—and that means no more nonsense.

No more hiding the little sins in our lives. No more hiding who we are right now, and who we want to become. No more hiding who we were, or putting on a show for others. No more settling for the show others give us. No more fake religion, or letting words flutter around us without examining our own hearts. No more walls that keep us in and everyone else out. No more games. No more running from problems and situations. No more rumours and ducking around corners instead of dealing with issues and accusations head on. No more ignoring the hard questions or belittling the gnawing little ones.

Start being who you are. Really. That's the only way you'll start to grow.

Many years ago, C. S. Lewis wrote an allegory of the story of Cupid called *Till We Have Faces*. Near the end of the book is one of my favourite passages of all literary work. The main character, Orual, says:

> I saw well why the gods do not speak to us openly, nor let us answer. Till the word can be dug out of us, why should they hear the babble that we think we mean? How can they meet us face to face till we have faces?[4]

CHAPTER THREE

JEREMIAH

B oxes are interesting things.
When I bought my house, the previous owner left two wooden boxes he had made in the house for us. He used to sell these boxes to funeral homes as urns for $100+ each.

I once accompanied a man who was transporting a couple of six-foot boxes to a crematorium.

We see boxes everywhere. They are used in our homes to pack or store things, and are especially useful when moving. Even when an object is round or oddly shaped, if it is put into a box, it becomes manageable. We are able to stack boxes and put them in rows. We may sacrifice some space by using boxes, but because they are so easily organized it's worth it.

Cats seem to really enjoy boxes, as long as it is their own idea. But the minute we try to force one of these furry creatures to be cute and cram it into a box, it leaps for freedom. Grasshoppers do the same, as do chickens, rabbits, puppies, and children. Adults especially seem to hate the idea of being trapped in a box. Even though boxes are exceptionally useful to organize and manage things, it seems no *living* thing or person has any interest in being put into one.

Only non-living things belong in boxes.

The Living God doesn't belong in a box.

Take, for example, this passage in Jeremiah 3:19, where God says:

> *I myself said, 'How gladly would I treat you like my children and give you a pleasant land, the most beautiful inheritance of any nation.' I thought you would call me 'Father' and not turn away from following me.* (NIV)

Don't rush past this—soak it in. Normally when reading something like that, I will begin jumping to conclusions or attempt to explain away what the passage says, but when I just let it say what it says, it changes me. This passage seems to say that God had made a prediction and was later shown to be wrong. How is this possible, what does this mean, where does this come from, and what are we supposed to do with this? It is an incredibly troubling passage because it is in complete contrast to what we have been taught about God. Before we dive into another translation to figure out how it "should" have been translated, consider what this might mean if it is revealed to be accurate. What does it mean for God to have had one idea and it not come true?

When you have grown up going to church and studying the Bible in college, it is incredibly easy for everything to simply become an academic pursuit. The Bible becomes a textbook, God becomes a test subject, moral and ethical principles are a matter of grades, and even our lifestyles come into question as something to be considered in our academic careers. Knowledge and understanding become the highest and best attributes to strive for, and if Christianity or God are anything beyond that, they seem not to matter. But I don't think people in the academic world are the only ones to feel this way.

Over the past number of years, I've observed that, for one reason or another, Christianity has been reduced to a set of principles and ideologies. Consequently, despite what the Exodus reveals, Christianity has been formed into a theory of how to manipulate God—either through a type of prayer formula, a salvation and rule methodology, or even through our basic understanding of Him. A shift has taken place whereby we try to put God into such academic terms that God has become limited by those definitions. Though not bluntly stated, the basic principle that this has produced is "Disregard what doesn't make sense to you." This results in a god who is limited and bound by the principles that are attributed to him by a people who cannot make sense of that which is beyond them.

We have, practically speaking, placed God inside a box—inside a box of infinity. He has no hopes or dreams, He doesn't ever change His mind because He knows everything and has predetermined actions like some sort of algorithm in a super computer. He never steps outside of the boundaries of infinity. And though there may be some truth to this, we really don't know what infinity looks like, do we? Thus, we gather all the knowledge and understanding we can, figure out the concepts to the best of our ability, disregard the matters that don't seem to make sense, formulate the rules and standards, and place God inside that limited understanding. In an attempt to understand God, humanity has reduced Him to a theory, or maybe simply a non-living thing inside a box.

I think it all comes down to a matter of control. If we can predict the consequences of a particular action, in a way we can control the situation, but if we can't understand completely the action-consequence relationship, we cannot accurately predict the outcome. For example, because we understand gravity on earth, we know that if we throw a ball it will eventually come back down. We can actually predict the results of gravity so well that we can throw a ball in such a way that it will land exactly where we want it to. However, if gravity was less predictable, one would feel less in control of the situation and would be less likely to throw a ball, because it would be unclear what would happen.

Thus, in an attempt to gain some level of control over God and the nature of the universe, despite often being quite oblivious to our own actions and motives, we have simplified Him to an object, law, or rule. Rather than get to know Him as He really is, we have treated God not as a Him, but as an it.

As we look to the passage in Jeremiah 3:19, the sentence that concerns us is *"I thought you would call me 'Father' and not turn away from following me"* (NIV).

As an object, principle, thing, law, or rule, this calls into question the very foundation of an infinite nature. How could God have been wrong about this? How could He have thought that one thing would happen, and then something else actually took place? Either God is not all-knowing, or... or, maybe God isn't a thing!

In this passage, God is speaking to His people, crying out to them. If we could have heard the tone of voice used, I imagine we would have heard pain and frustration. We would have recognized sadness and passion. I think we would have felt the pain of a hope not realized—a hope from someone who knew what would happen, knew what was going to come about, but wanted something different anyway.

When I was in college, a professor from another school came to teach a one-week intensive seminar on the book of Jeremiah. It was a seminar that changed my life—an investigation into a book that consistently makes me uncomfortable and amazed. During the seminar, the professor had us look at this passage and then gave us this analogy:

If there are any women in the class who have watched Titanic more than once, you will understand what it means to know the ending, and still hope that it doesn't happen.

He said "women" because they seem to carry this character-istic of hope more than men, though men have expressed it as well. His point was, though, that God hopes despite His knowledge. It means that God cannot be limited by a finite understanding of infinity, by the expression of Him as an object, or bound up in rules and laws as if they are what He is based on. God is not based on rules. Remarkably, God cannot be put into a box, even if that box is one of infinity, if it would reduce Him to a being who is all-knowing and all-powerful and so cannot hope. God must be more than that. He cannot be reduced to an "it" or simply a "thing"—He must be a person.

A.W. Tozer saw this years ago. In his book *The Pursuit of God* he wrote:

> We have almost forgotten that God is a person and, as such, can be cultivated as any person can. It is inherent in personality to be able to know other personalities, but full knowledge of one personality by another cannot be achieved in one encounter. It is only after long and loving mental intercourse that the full possibilities of both can be explored.[5]

We cannot have a relationship with a rock, a desk, a computer, a dress, a stick, or an action figure. We may be able to change how we act around them, or because they exist, we may change our behaviour, modify our perspective, adjust our value structure, or rethink how we invest in other areas, but we cannot have a relationship with them. To interact, there must be action on both sides, hence "inter-act." Walking by a jacket in a store may make us want to buy it, wear it, act a certain way in it, use it to attain status or attention or some kind of self-fulfillment, but there is no interaction going on. Yes, we may have trouble putting it on, but that is simply an attempt to dance around and control an object that is impersonal, inanimate, and unable to interact itself. In this same way, if God is an impersonal being, religion and Christianity are just a game.

In studying Jeremiah, several passages become obstacles to the thought that God functions as an object, or according to rules outside of Himself. In Jeremiah chapter 3, God tells the Israelites that according to the Law, once you were divorced and married to another you couldn't go back to your first spouse. God then tells Israel that they had divorced Him and been married to pagan idols, which would, according to the Law, mean that they could not go back to their first spouse: God. Yet, God calls them to come back to Him. God gives a law and then contradicts this law by His appeal to the people of Israel to come back.

Then there is Jeremiah 20, where Jeremiah flat out tells God that God deceived him and overpowered him. He calls out to God and tells Him that He is an abusive dictator. Then there is no response from God on this matter, and God does not punish Jeremiah for saying it. It is simply stated as part of Jeremiah's rant and left alone.

In Jeremiah 18:5–10, God describes how the world works. God says that He has one set of plans, and depending on how we react, those plans get changed! He describes how if He has good in store for someone, but they reject Him and His ways, the good plans will disappear and bad plans will be put in their place. God says that if He has bad plans in store for someone, but they turn towards Him and humble themselves to His will, the bad plans will be changed to good plans. Actually, the word used in verse 8 (NIV) is "relent." The Hebrew word used is *nacham*, which can be translated "to be sorry," "repent," or "comfort."[6] God says He will change His mind and be sorry for what He had planned.

Upon reading this it is very tempting for me to come up with two, maybe three, solutions to these issues. I think, "It is simply a matter of context and once I look at the entire passage and situation there won't be anything shocking." Or I start blaming the translation of the text. I may wonder if this is just a matter of describing God in finite terms, and if due to our limited language, this is the best way we have to describe an infinite God. But when I look again at these passages, it becomes clear that those are just my cop-outs, my excuses for keeping God in a box. Instead of allowing my already formed beliefs and assumptions to develop how I understand the passages, I need to allow the passages to develop my beliefs.

We are told that God is all-knowing, all-powerful, all-present, present in all time, unlimited, infinite. We take this information and we apply it so completely to all of our beliefs and interpretations that when we read anything concerning God and His interaction with the world and people, He simply becomes the personification of rules and theories. He becomes a being that is unknowable. He becomes the regulatory factor and "thing" that guards and organizes the universe. He is akin to the laws of physics, except more important. Through these lenses He is predictable, controllable, and a perfectly inanimate thing.

I am not saying this to argue against His characteristics of being all-knowing and all-powerful, or any of the other infinite descriptions found in the first sentence of the previous paragraph. I say this because those things have erroneously become definitions rather than characteristics of God. That is why these passages in Jeremiah are so essential:

Jeremiah 3 describes how God isn't bound by laws, but is the creator of them, and so is willing to go beyond them in order to reach those He loves.

Jeremiah 18 reveals a kind of give-and-take sovereignty that isn't based upon flat dictation, but an all-powerful being that allows the will of finite beings to influence Him and the world.

Jeremiah 20 shows God's ability to take honesty, work with it, and give grace to those who want to talk and vent and argue and yell.

We look at these chapters, trying to wrap our heads around them, but there is just one honest answer that can explain and express what they reveal about God. There is only one solution, only one idea that can make any sense of what these texts express:

God is a living person.

If we want to get really technical, He is actually three persons, one being: Trinity.

Which means He is personal. He has a personality.

If I am being honest, this is a terrifying concept. I read through these thoughts, examine the texts, and I know that there is no real contradiction. I know the text is true, and the enormous reality is that God is far beyond my comprehension, yet completely relevant. He doesn't fit the rules I grew up on, and He doesn't fit the form and boundaries that I had previously set, or even the lines I am comfortable with.

In dealing with people who have their own thoughts, desires, and personalities, it quickly becomes apparent that they cannot be controlled or understood very easily. How much more, then, is the daunting reality of God? If God is not simply rules, but is personal, He ceases to be as predictable as we would like. He reveals dynamics and aspects of His being which go beyond what we understand, and consequently make it impossible for us to scientifically predict and control Him.

This isn't to say that God is sporadic or some sort of manic personality that makes decisions arbitrarily without reason or thought, which are faulty traits of human personalities, not God. It is to say that there is more to Him than is understandable and controllable by human logic, science (by which I mean the method of repetition and analysis), and manipulation. If God is personal, I am much smaller than I had previously guessed.

There are two big theological words that we use when we give God human-like attributes or traits (like, "the *hand* of God" or "God was *angry*")—anthropomorphism and anthropopathism. I don't want you to confuse what I'm saying with those concepts. I'm not saying that God has a personality like we have a personality. I'm not saying that God gets angry like we get angry. I'm not saying that God is like us. What I *am* saying is that we are like God. We aren't giving God human-like attributes, we are recognizing God's attributes in us.

Our emotions, personalities, ideas, abilities, creativity, and dreams are all based on His emotions, personality, ideas, abilities, creativity, and dreams. We are a derivative of Him, not Him of us. He is the first, and then we came from that. I'm not saying we are God, or are part of God, or are made of the same substance as God or something ridiculous like that. What I'm saying is that God took the pattern of Himself and created beings from that pattern, much as we would with a car schematic or wedding dress design. When looking at a veil, or a train, they look like they came from something designed after a wedding gown. When looking at a fender, or a steering wheel, they look like something designed after a car. We also look like what we've been modeled after.

He is infinite (unlimited) and complete. We are finite (limited) and broken. He is perfect and we are not. We are but a dark reflection of His radiant image. Our attributes are based on His, not vice-versa. His personality is what ours are based on, finite and broken as they are.

Perhaps a better analogy would be a photograph. When we take a picture of a person, we capture in the photograph a single, momentary, finite, image of a living person. The picture isn't that person, it doesn't have the same value as that person, nor is it able to do the things that person is able to, but it does reflect something of that person. We simply have an extremely small expression of who that person is—and often such expressions are cherished because of who they reflect. This is quite similar to who we are in relation to who God is. If we are dynamic, incredible persons, how much more so is God?

This is an incredible idea, but more than that, I think it is an essential truth that we can't forget or ignore. The fact that God has a personality is one of the most essential ideas in the Christian faith. If God isn't a person, then we aren't really able to have a relationship with Him, and our entire concept of salvation is but a façade for a grandiose legal loophole. If God isn't a person, we cannot relate to Him, nor He to us. It is but a cold and dead organization of rules, stipulations, and formulas, just like that of all the other pagan belief systems that are based on inanimate objects, shaped and crafted by man, and fitted nicely into a box.

Having grown up in the Church, this chapter messes with my head. Even as I write it, I find myself questioning and being challenged by the concepts expressed here. But regardless of how troubling they are, and how far beyond my ability to fully comprehend, I believe them to be absolutely essential to the matter of God and humanity. Because if God is to be the point from which we understand everything else, He cannot be limited by any box I put Him in.

Yes, I already thought that God was a person—I sang about that in many church songs—but I don't think I really believed it. Maybe you can relate to that too. Maybe there are times we still aren't sure if we really believe it.

If we really did believe it, we would act a lot differently. Instead of a shallow and fragmented ideology and tradition, Christianity would be about getting to know, being known by, talking with, hearing from, following, petitioning, and discussing with God. It would be about falling in love, going through conflicts, and arguing with God. It would be about being disciplined by God, celebrating with God, and living like God would live if He were a finite, limited, human being.

Instead, it looks more like a bunch of people trying to find a magic formula that releases a coveted mixture of moral, social, psychological, and mental freedoms and powers which will allow them to be in control. Sadly, more often than not, I've prayed because I knew I should, not because I wanted to know God. We live obediently and go to church on Sundays because we want to ensure we get to paradise when we die, not because we just want to be closer to the One who made us and will fight for us. We so often sing the songs, pay our tithes, help the poor, serve in different ministries, clean up garbage off the streets, and forgive those who have wronged us because that's what we've been told will result in a happier life, not because we want to be more like the One we admire, look up to, and come from.

If God is a person, Christianity should be just like getting to know someone. In the same way we build a relationship with another human, we need to work to build a relationship with a being, a person, who is even more of a person and has a more perfect and full personality than we do. To build relationships, we have to spend time with people and get to know their facial expressions, tone, habits, ideas, vocabulary, the sound of their voice, the meaning of certain grimaces, sighs, grunts, eye-rolls, and body language. In like manner, we have to get to know God.

Imagine your relationships with the people around you. Think about how much conflict, joy, interaction, unpredictability, and creativity are involved in those relationships. Think about how you get to know one another. Think about how you have good days and bad days together—some of which you go through together, others of which you go through *because* you are together. Think about the little conversations you have with each other, how sometimes you fly off the handle, and how with some you can be brutally honest and vent without fear that they will retaliate, because you know they understand you just need to vent. Think about the feeling of falling in love with someone you can't control and dominate, because they are more than you. Think about how you grow closer and closer until your only desire is to know them inside out.

Does that sound like the Christianity you know? Does that sound like your relationship with God? Does that even sound possible?

When I read Jeremiah, and now the entire Biblical text, I am convinced this is the point. Actually, Jesus makes a statement that says it plainly: *"Now this is eternal life: that they know you, the only true God, and Jesus Christ, whom you have sent"* (John 17:3, NIV).

In a world dying of loneliness, insincerity, fear, and greed, perhaps what we need most is to know, and be known by, this personal God.

This is no longer about laws, rules, dogmas, or even science. It's about the question that Moses asked while standing beside a burning bush. It isn't about what we come from, or what we are, or what we must become.

It's about the question, "*Who* is this living God?"

CHAPTER FOUR

TRINITY

One of my favourite genres of TV show, film or literature is the whodunnit mystery. Shows like *Matlock*, *Murder, She Wrote*, *JAG*, *CSI*, and *Scooby-Doo* all have the element of trying to find the truth, and ultimately finding the person they were looking for. The original *CSI* ran its opening credits to a song called "Who Are You?" There's just something captivating about trying to discover the person whom all the evidence points to, and it's almost like the mystery compels us to go on the search.

So, here we are. Who is the living God?

Well, first we need to accept that if we can fully understand God, we've probably made Him up. The God that is alive, and accordingly doesn't fit into a box, must be beyond us.

We need to accept that we will never completely understand God. Who He is, how He is, what He is made of—it's all a mystery, and that mystery compels us to go on the search. But as humans we just can't wrap our brains around all that He is and how He is able to work the way He does, at least not completely.

Please don't confuse this initial statement with a cop-out. To dig into the question of God, we simply must begin with the realization that if we could fully understand God, it would be likely that He was just a human creation. Creatures don't fully comprehend their Creator. If God is our creator, there will always be an aspect of mystery. If we conclude that we have understood God completely, we either have discovered that He is manmade, have become greater than God, don't know as much as we think we do, or have discovered something other than God. Thus, if we're truly to know this God we've been talking about, the God of the Exodus, we must resolve ourselves to the fact that we will never have all the answers. We can know Him, yes, absolutely—but we will never know Him better than He knows Himself, or have the kind of knowledge that brings us power over Him. He is God and we are not.

With that resolution comes a necessary task: faith.

We must make a choice whether we will believe and submit to someone we cannot fully understand, or not. We must choose whether there is a being greater than us, that we cannot control or have power over and thus must submit to, or not.

Perhaps you aren't ready for that yet. Maybe you want to think and search more before you decide how you want to approach this idea of God. If that's the case, I would ask that you read with an open mind as we will continue into the depths of the persons of God, all the while remembering that there will always be some mystery involved. But one day, everyone will have to choose.

Now, that being said, we can continue the search for the One that all the evidence points to. We must get all the answers we can, even if some things will remain beyond us.

In keeping with the mysterious nature of God, we know that He is one being and three persons.

Not three beings.

Not one person with multiple personalities.

One being, three persons. In Matthew 3:15–17, during the baptism of Jesus, all three persons are present simultaneously, and in Matthew 28:19, Jesus instructs his followers, *"Therefore go*

and make disciples of all nations, baptizing them in the name of
the Father and of the Son and of the Holy Spirit..." (NIV).

The term "Trinity" comes from "tri," meaning three, and
"unity," meaning one. Each person of the Trinity is unique, and
each is fully God. We will come back to the dynamics of this at the
end of this chapter, but what I would like to investigate currently
is less of an ontological or philosophical perspective and more of
a personal/relational view. Let's meet the three persons, God the
Father, God the Son, and God the Holy Spirit.

FATHER

In the Old Testament, the Father was the person of the Trinity
that was most apparent. There the world caught a glimpse of the
God of the Exodus; the God who is greater and more powerful
than any other thing or person in the universe.

Genesis says that God created all that was and is in six days.
It was a remarkable genius speaking into existence the very idea,
concept, and physical being of light, stars, planets, animals, water, plants, atmosphere, and even mankind—all out of nothing.
We know from studying other parts of the Bible that God is completely self-sufficient, not needing anyone or anything. Yet despite this complete independence, He sought to create, to make
something outside of Himself.

God has a will and He wanted to create—to express and expand and share. 1 John 4:16 says that *"God is love"* (NIV). The Greek
word John uses is *agape*, which has a particular force behind it.
Unlike our English use of the word "love," describing anything
from sex to tacos, the Greeks had multiple words to describe different forms of love. *Agape* describes a completely selfless love,
a giving of self without thought of reciprocation. It is completely vulnerable in giving itself, and it doesn't give in order to get
something back. *Agape* describes God and expresses the root of
creation. He created something completely other than Himself,

yet wove aspects of His own character into creation, even creating humanity in His own image.

Everything was designed to function as God does in *agape*. According to their initial design and purpose, everything in creation would work to serve and bless the other aspects of creation. There was no selfishness, no greed, no hatred, and no death. Creation was to be completely sustained by giving without thought of return. It was perfect... until humanity decided they wanted something different.

Humans, alone out of all the created things, had the ability to make a choice. This made humanity able to love in free will as God loves rather than simply as a programmed response. God gave humanity an opportunity to be *like* Him, but they decided they wanted to *be* Him instead. Humans didn't want to be the created *image* of God, they wanted to be *God*.

Humans in their purest form are not selfish, and so in our act of greed we were changed from the image of God into something less. We became sub-human. In a world created to reflect *agape*, we now pursued sin, selfishness, lust, pride, power, and evil. Our choice broke us, and tainted the rest of creation.

God built creation to be sustained by love. If humanity's selfishness remained unchecked, creation would suffer the resulting pain of abuse and death. Having every reason to get rid of this destructive creature, God chose not to. It would have made sense to rid the earth of the being that wasn't working like it was designed to, the thing causing damage to the rest of creation. Like removing cancer from a healthy body, it would have been logical to simply remove humanity from an otherwise healthy creation. And yet, God didn't. Instead, God set a plan into motion to repair the damage and restore what had been lost.

This plan involved the will of humanity, and God gave humanity another choice to make. He said, "Follow me, or you will die," which subtly implies two significant things. Just like in the Exodus, God initiated the reconnection and opened the door before any love could be earned. It also means that if we seek our own desires instead of reflecting God's *agape* love, there are consequences. This leads us to a necessary insight into our relationship with God the Father: love is unconditional, but relationship isn't, and relationship is life.

Love is unconditional, but relationship isn't.

Agape pours out love and blessing, but if the conditions of relationship are not met, they have no application.

Isn't that a contradiction? I don't think so. Love is the first. It is there before anything else takes place. Regardless of our actions or reactions, love is there in fullness. All actions and thoughts come after it. Nothing we do or say can make God love us, or make Him give us love or not love us. He loves us. That is first and last, and we have no power over that. We do, however, have a part to play in the relationship, and if God is personal, as discussed in the previous chapter, then we must agree that we can have a relationship with Him. If so, we must say that this relationship, like every other relationship in our lives, has certain conditions.

If you love someone, but they don't love you back, there is no relationship.

If a man loves his wife, and she runs off with another man, there is a broken relationship.

If a man loves a woman, and she isn't interested and actually avoids him, he might be a stalker, but there is still no relationship.

You get the picture.

Luke 15:11–32 records a story told by Jesus commonly referred to as the Prodigal Son. It is the story of a young man who takes his inheritance and wastes it. His father knows his son has been foolish, but when he finally returns home, the father welcomes him with open arms. In this story, the father always loves his son, but when the son leaves, there is no relationship, no affection, no care, no benefit. Only when the son returns home is the relationship restored.

We have all rejected God, and so sought to destroy His creation, and He has sought to save us, to restore the relationship, to share His selfless blessing again—but that relationship is conditional upon our acceptance of it.

These characteristics are expressed and fleshed out in great detail throughout the scriptures. It is the story of how God set out to love and restore a broken relationship, and restore humanity to what it was meant to be! This should give us a starting point as we reflect on who the Father really is in later chapters.

SON

The Son is the person of the Trinity that is most apparent in the New Testament Gospels; we know Him as Jesus.

Our first encounter with Jesus is not in the Gospels, however. There is evidence of Him in several sections of the Old Testament. One is at the attempt to burn three men in a fiery furnace (Daniel 3). There is also an implicit mention of Jesus, as well as the Holy Spirit, in Genesis 1 when God speaks in the plural personal pronoun "us." John then speaks to this in the first chapter of his Gospel.

> *In the beginning was the Word, and the Word was with God, and the Word was God. He was in the beginning with God. All things were made through him, and without him was not any thing made that was made. In him was life, and the life was the light of men. The light shines in the darkness, and the darkness has not overcome it.*
>
> *There was a man sent from God, whose name was John. He came as a witness, to bear witness about the light, that all might believe through him. He was not the light, but came to bear witness about the light.*
>
> *The true light, which gives light to everyone, was coming into the world. He was in the world, and the world was made through him, yet the world did not know him. He came to his own, and his own people did not receive him. But to all who did receive him, who believed in his*

name, he gave the right to become children of God, who were born, not of blood nor of the will of the flesh nor of the will of man, but of God.

And the Word became flesh and dwelt among us, and we have seen his glory, glory as of the only Son from the Father, full of grace and truth.

—John 1:1–14, ESV

In order to understand the Gospels, you must first understand that Jesus is God. The work Jesus did on Earth was remarkable, but realizing that He is God makes it less about doing something impressive and more about turning the world upside down. Take a moment to reread the above passage. It speaks of God becoming human—the fullness of God becoming fully human.

Consider what the previous section discussed concerning the character and being of God the Father, the God of the Exodus. The great, holy, powerful, omniscient, omnipotent, omnipresent, infinite, and awesome creator of all things became the creation. The creator became one of the creatures. That's like a human becoming a computer, or a dress, or a painting. To give up the fullness of one's being to become something so limited, fragile, and small is ridiculous. And yet this is what John says Jesus did! Paul echoes this when he says:

When the time came, he set aside the privileges of deity and took on the status of a slave, became human*! Having become human, he stayed human. It was an incredibly humbling process. He didn't claim special privileges. Instead, he lived a selfless, obedient life and then died a selfless, obedient death—and the worst kind of death at that—a crucifixion.*

—Philippians 2:7–8, MSG (emphasis in original)

Even before we dive into the life, death, resurrection, and mission of Jesus, we need to deal with what it means for God to have become a man. This was the greatest and most necessary sacrifice made by God. I'm not just speaking from a linear perspective that says, "If Jesus hadn't come as a man, then He wouldn't have been able to die and rise again and so resolve the sin issue." No, as true as that is, the necessity and enormity of the situation is found squarely in the act of the incarnation itself. When God became a man, something came into being that hadn't existed since the time of the first humans in creation: a human with the full, unbroken, image of God.

For the first time since Adam and Eve had chosen to reject their ingrained image and purpose of *agape*, there was a human who was complete, as He was intended to be. God had set His nature inside of man once again. Man with no sin, man with no need to die, man without selfishness and hatred, man with love and grace and purpose. Who Jesus *was* is who we were meant to be. How He lived, acted, and thought is how we were meant to.

God brought His image back to mankind. Through the sacrifice of Jesus becoming human, God was beginning a new stage in His work to restore His creation. Jesus, the Saviour of humanity, called the Christ, would have to go through incredible things in order to bring this image back to us. He would have to live our life and die our death so we could live His life. He would have to walk our path so that we could then walk His.

Jesus lived on the earth for about thirty-three years, and went through all of the trials and temptations that we face. He was tempted to use His abilities in order to cheat and make Himself happy rather than fight for others. He was tempted by women and wealth. He was tempted to test God's love for Him. I think Jesus was even tempted to doubt His own identity, a temptation many, if not all of us, face (Matthew 4:1–11). And yet, in everything, Jesus never once gave into the temptation, and never once sinned. In every situation and circumstance, Jesus lived according to the image of God. He was who we were meant to be.

But then humans saw something powerful and wanted that power themselves, as humans always do. John 11:46–50 implies that the Pharisees weren't simply angry with what Jesus was saying, but knew who Jesus was and so wanted to kill Him because He would harm their way of life. These men had their eyes opened enough to know something that only the disciple Peter saw, and instead of submitting and following God incarnate, they saw Him as a threat to their traditions and lifestyles, and killed Him.

Then on the third day, He rose from the dead in such a complete victory over death that it would never hold power over Him again. Jesus remains alive even today. (More on this in later chapters.)

This man who lived without sin, fully in the image of God, defeated death. He followed our path from birth to death, and then set a new course for us. God became man to reset the course, just like a great 4x4 truck driving down a muddy dirt road filled with deep ruts can create a new set of ruts for all other vehicles to follow in.

But the work wasn't done, because Jesus didn't come to just show us how great He was and how greatly we had failed. He wanted to actually change things. He wanted to redeem and remake humans. And so, to complete this work He had to leave and send the Holy Spirit, who would make His work a reality in every life that would follow Him and His Kingdom.

HOLY SPIRIT

The Holy Spirit is the person of the Trinity that is most apparent in the New Testament after the Gospel accounts, and whose work continues presently.

In the book of Acts, Jesus spoke to His disciples and then ascended into heaven. This is a mysterious event, because we know that heaven isn't actually physically above us like the sky is, but somehow He transitioned into another realm. Before that happened, though, He said, *"Unless I go away, the Advocate will not come to you; but if I go, I will send him to you"* (John 16:7, NIV).

That's an incredible statement! Jesus basically says, "I am going so you can have the Holy Spirit." The Holy Spirit is present throughout the Old and New Testament, which makes sense because the Trinity comprises three persons at the same time. They aren't some shifting god caught in an identity crisis. Yet, His full outpouring is at Pentecost.

There is a single key aspect we must examine as we get to know God and as we come to understand the symmetry of God and creation: the re-application of the image of God to humanity.

The work of Jesus in becoming human and living out the image of God would only change us if God applied it to us. So, God sent the Holy Spirit to give us the life of Christ. The work of Christ had to be accomplished before the Holy Spirit could fall on us. When the Spirit comes upon a person, Jesus' death becomes their death, and His life becomes their life! When the Holy Spirit comes upon a person, the new self is born.

This is what Jesus was speaking about in John 3 when He said that we must all be born again, made brand new. The Holy Spirit would come on us with the power, victory, life, and freedom of Christ. This would result not just in humans being free from the power of sin and death, but humans living the life of Christ—humans living like Jesus—humans re-made in the image of God—humans living and being in such a way that when others looked at them, they would be reminded of God and give Him glory (see Matthew 5:16).

He did this in the New Testament, and He is still doing it today.

TRINITY

Three different persons, one being, working throughout creation and history in order to express Themselves and bless Their creation. As Wolfhart Pannenburg writes, "From all eternity the Father loves the Son, the Son loves the Father, and the Spirit loves the Father in the Son and the Son in the Father. Each of the trinitarian persons loves the other, the Father the Son, the Son the Father, the Spirit both in fellowship."[7] If this is correct, I offer the following diagram for all of us visual learners.

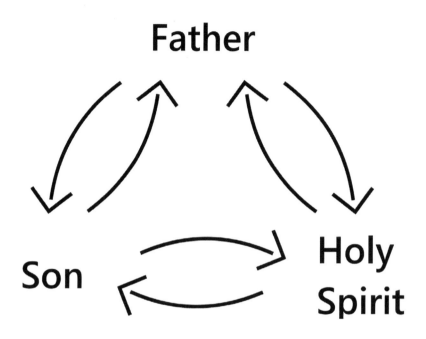

The arrows represent *agape* love, a love that gives and gives without thought of what it will get back. We know from 1 John 4 that God is love. We also know from Scripture that God is one, and yet three persons. Here we see how this dynamic works. Each person of the Trinity pours out their love completely to the others. This leaves no one out. Each person is continually and fully given the blessing, love, attention, and focus of the others, all contained within a single being: God. This produces unlimited amounts of love, and makes God the only being that can love with *agape* all on His own, without any requirement of any outside being.

Agape needs to give and to love, which is why we require others to express *agape* love. *Agape* cannot be the love of the self; it must be the love of others. Since God is three persons, one being,

He loves another while it remains inside of His own being. No other being is like this. This is how *agape* can be present in His being, with no actual need of any other being. This is the nature of God, and in the following pages we will see how this is the basis for our design as well.

CHAPTER FIVE

DIAGRAMS OF GOD & MAN

This chapter is full of diagrams and short explanations for each one. I hope it will lead to many questions, and some clarity. It isn't my intention in this book to provide all the answers, and it especially isn't my intention in this chapter to fully express the ideas behind each of these diagrams. Much of the rest of this book will flesh out and explain these pictures in greater detail and increasing relevance to Christianity, our world, and our lives.

I am a visual learner and have found that these diagrams set the stage for much of the theology and philosophy I hold to. They aren't meant to be legalistic or absolute—they are simply expressions of a world I am beginning to understand, and I hope they will be of help to you. Who God is shows us who we were meant to be, and who He sent the Holy Spirit to make us into.

So God created man in his own image, in the image of God he created him; male and female he created them.
—Genesis 1:27, ESV

Then the Lord God said, "It is not good that the man should be alone; I will make him a helper fit for him."
—Genesis 2:18, ESV

You were taught, with regard to your former way of life, to put off your old self, which is being corrupted by its deceitful desires; to be made new in the attitude of your minds; and to put on the new self, created to be like God in true righteousness and holiness.
—Ephesians 4:22–24, NIV

Therefore be imitators of God, as beloved children. And walk in love, as Christ loved us and gave himself up for us, a fragrant offering and sacrifice to God.
—Ephesians 5:1–2, ESV

Do not lie to each other, since you have taken off your old self with its practices and have put on the new self, which is being renewed in knowledge in the image of its Creator.
—Colossians 3:9–10, NIV

And we all, who with unveiled faces contemplate the Lord's glory, are being transformed into his image with ever-increasing glory, which comes from the Lord, who is the Spirit.
—2 Corinthians 3:18, NIV

Whoever claims to live in him must live as Jesus did.
—1 John 2:6, NIV

The command we have from Christ is blunt: Loving God includes loving people. You've got to love both.
—1 John 4:21, MSG

God

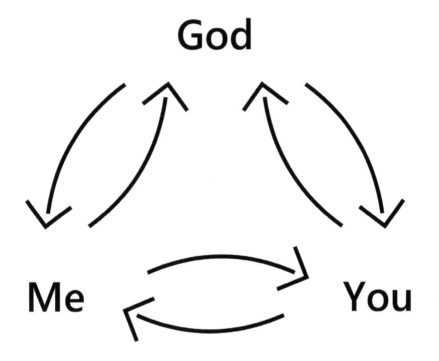

Me   You

We see here how we were meant to be. God, who is love, sends us love, and we are supposed to give it back to Him. This is what we would call worship. He loves us, so we love Him more, and then He sends us more love, and we send more back to Him, and then we share it with each other. He pours out love to us, and we are supposed to send it back to Him in worship. Then, because He has loved us, we are to love each other.

As it should be apparent, when we love in this manner, with this *agape* between you, me, and God, we find a similar design to that of the inner workings of the Trinity. We were meant to reflect that nature. Just look at the commands God gave us in the book of Genesis to take care of the earth, to multiply, to watch over the plants and animals (Genesis 1:28). We were not designed to remain in ourselves; we were created to love those outside of ourselves. To love God and love others is why we are here (Matthew 22:36–40). This is what we were created to be in the Garden of Eden, before the fall of man. God made man, He saw that man needed another outside of himself to love, and so He created woman (Genesis 2:18–25). He formed a relationship between Himself, man, and woman as a reflection of the inner workings of the Trinity. It is the image of God presented through human beings.

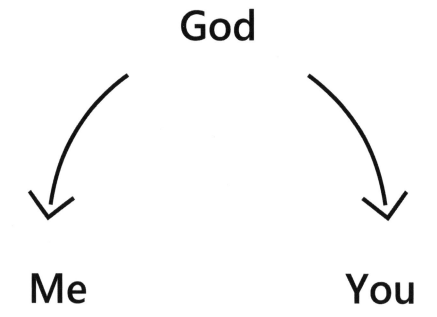

God

Me   You

Ever since the fall of man, this is how life has started for each and every human being, save Jesus—as we saw in the last chapter. Being broken humans, fallen from the glory and image of God, we naturally take love and try to keep it to ourselves. We don't give it back to God, and we don't share it with others. It is selfish, petty, and useless. In doing this, we may have our needs taken care of to a certain extent, but in that state we are subhuman, less than the image of God, and we know it. It is death. We feel it deep down, and constantly crave something else. It is the reason advertising campaigns are so effective, and why war is so inevitable.

Yet, even though it is a dead state, there are three things to take note of: 1) God initiates the process and makes His love available; 2) God loves others just as much, and as often, as He loves us; 3) He loves others even before we love ourselves or love others. He is the key to anything changing. Without His initial love, everything we do lacks worth and substance. If He didn't take the first step in pouring out His love, we would have no love to give or share. It's only through His unconditional love that anything is ever able to change.

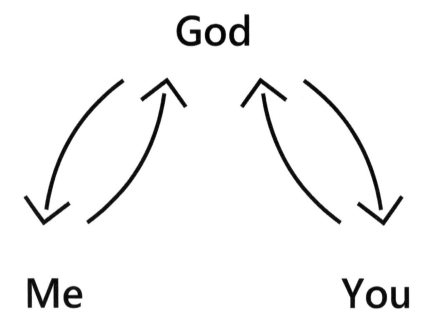

God

Me   You

At first glance this diagram may seem to be good and valuable; however, it isn't. Though there are pieces of the image that are present, one central aspect is absent. When we compare the love between the three persons of the Trinity and the love between God and humanity, we notice that there is a relationship missing here. The reciprocating arrows express a relationship of *agape* giving from both sides. One-way love isn't a relationship. Without the relationship between humans, we aren't living as God lives, we aren't loving as God loves, and so we aren't expressing His image.

Simply read through the books of the prophets in Scripture, and you will find that God consistently calls the people to stop trying to "worship" Him if they are just going to neglect their fellow human beings (Isaiah 58). God actually calls it insulting for people to act like they love God without loving their neighbours (1 John 4:20). It doesn't reflect who He is, even though many would claim it does. God says in the Scriptures that He would rather us feed the poor, correct injustices, and forgive debts than just pretend to be holy and worship Him (Hosea 6:6). To neglect our neighbours and then "worship" God isn't His image, it isn't love, and it isn't good. It is fake.

This diagram is actually impossible. We may think this happens, and may see people trying to live this way, but in reality, if people are not loving as God loves—in His image, vertically and horizontally—they aren't loving God.

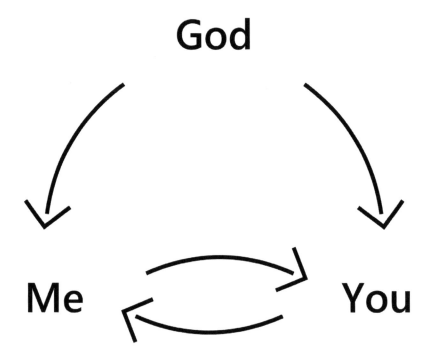

In the early twenty-first century, we find this picture happening a lot. However, it's just as impossible as the previous diagram. At least, it's impossible for the arrows to take on the representation of *agape*. It may be some kind of love, but it isn't *agape*. It is tainted and shallow love—love that lacks the potency and purity that changes lives and creates life. Yes, God is sending us His love, but until that love is returned and a relationship is established, it has very little effect on us. Our attempts to love will remain broken and limited. We will think that "rights" are what love looks like, and that freedom to do whatever we want without judgment is love. Without an established relationship with God, our attempts to love will be worthless.

We see this in the great debates over sexuality, alcohol, drugs, and religion. Many argue that love deems all things acceptable as long as we are looking out for the freedoms of our fellow humans. Yet if one follows this argument to its logical conclusion, it becomes obvious that freedom may be nice to think about but very painful when faced with its consequences.

Love must contain truth and discipline. It must be based on God's love, *agape*, or else it will be worthless. It must have elements of *truth* and *experience* (more on this later).

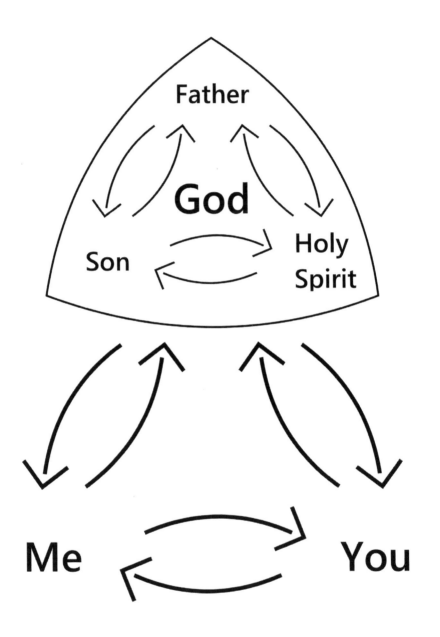

We are told that the Church is the Body of Christ, that it is the representation of God on earth (1 Corinthians 12). This is where we see the image of God displayed most fully and most passionately, or at least this is where it is supposed to be seen. I make this statement because it seems that what we have called "the Church" most often hasn't been in line with this diagram. In reality, if it does not fit this image, it isn't what the Church is supposed to be, and may not actually be "the Church" at all.

No group is perfect, but if it's going to carry the title of "Church" it should at least be attempting to reflect this design. When someone walks into a group of people who call themselves Christians, they should see and feel this diagram expressed.

This is the dynamic that pulls people into the faith and makes them want to be Christian, know more about God, and change. This is the way we were made to be, the way we were meant to function. It cries out to us when we see it and experience it. No gimmicks required: when people really see this, they will know deep down that this is how life was meant to be, and they will be drawn to it, called to it, and—if we are being the Church—loved into it.

As this diagram reflects the inner workings of the Church as it was designed to be as the Body of Christ, the image of God on earth, we can also quite easily replace "Me" with "Us" and "You" with "Them." It's not just you and me, it's my family and your family, my community and your community, our church and your church, us in our denomination and you in yours, all loving each other and loving God together in different places and different ways.

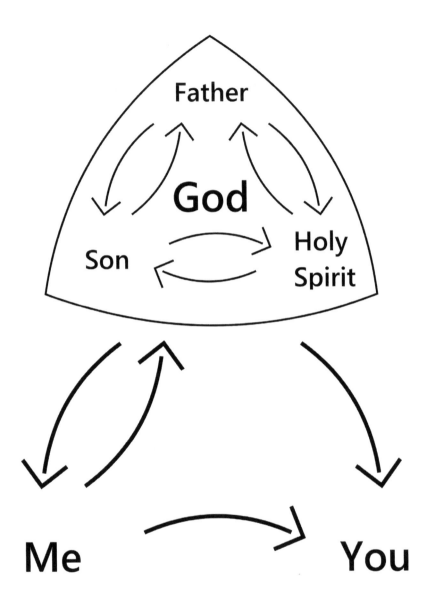

This is how we, as Christians and as the Church, must function. We can only ever ensure *our* part of the image of God. We are called to love God and love others, but we can't make others love God or love us. Though our ultimate desire is that others would love God, that the love we pour out to them would then be shared with others and would be sent back up to God, this isn't where we start. We start with glorifying God through living out His love in our lives, allowing Him to form the image in us. We then pour ourselves out to others in their need, failure, success, joy, sadness, gain, loss, strength, and weakness. We do our part.

At the same time, as we reach out, God is reaching out as well. In reality, God reaches out and works on those we are trying to love before we even get there, when we are there, and after we are gone. We aren't the essential factor in reaching people—God is. And still, He uses us to reflect His image to them in human form.

God loves, even if they don't deserve it. We must also love even though they don't deserve it. He cares for us physically, emotionally, spiritually, financially, vocationally, and in every other way. We must care for others physically, emotionally, spiritually, financially, vocationally, and in every other way. No matter the cost, we must reach out. That is love.

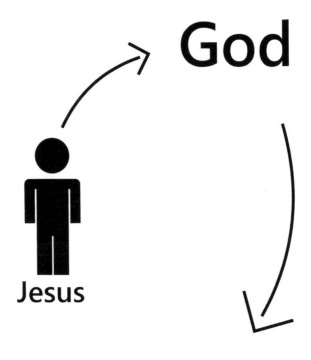

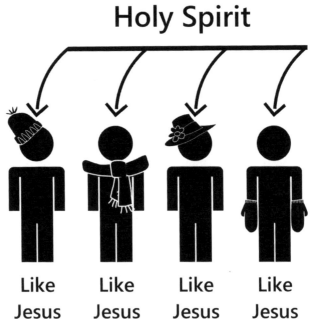

This is an exciting picture from Scripture. Jesus says in John 14 that He will leave the disciples so that He can send the Spirit and so they can do even greater things than He did when He was on earth. It is stressed throughout the Scriptures that the Spirit is available to anyone who will submit to Him (John 14:26, Acts 2:17, Acts 2:38, Romans 5:5, Romans 8:26). The Spirit makes the victory, power, purpose, and image of Christ (the image of God in the form of perfect humanity) available to each person who accepts Him. We can defeat sin because the Spirit in us is the Spirit of Christ who has already defeated sin! His victory is ours. His purpose and image become ours, because He is with us through the Spirit.

We are called The Body of Christ in 1 Corinthians 12. One of us plays one role, someone else a different role, but all who are in Christ reflect Him. Instead of there being one Jesus—one human image of God on earth—there can be many people like Jesus reflecting His image to the world. It doesn't make us God, but it restores the image of God. The Spirit makes us what we were meant to be. What Jesus alone could do on earth has been multiplied because His Body, His presence on earth, has increased and spread around the world through His people.

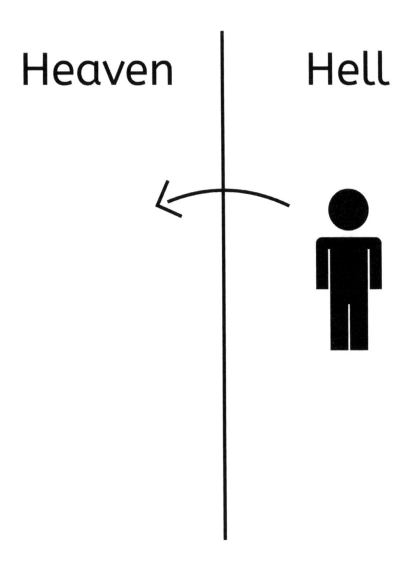

Heaven

Hell

This is basically the way salvation is taught today. There is a line between those going to heaven and those going to hell, and we are on one side or the other. Once we believe in the right thing and commit to it, then we're able to jump the line and join the other side. The act of salvation is then complete, and after this, we simply wait for the end. Yes, we're also told that if we love Jesus we will want to stop doing bad things, but that's really just a side-note tacked onto the idea that we are now on the safe side of the line. It's kind of like a spiritual and eternal version of tag where we want to get to the base to be safe.

The problem with this idea is that it's severely limited and inaccurate. It makes salvation into a single act that influences our future final location. It says nothing about what salvation does to us, how it changes us. It shows nothing of growth, and even makes growth insignificant—or at least makes it into an afterthought. *Where* we will spend eternity becomes the central point, rather than *how* we will spend eternity. And yes, there is a difference.

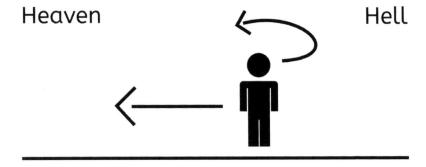

I propose that this is a more accurate illustration of the process, act, and purpose of salvation. Instead of salvation having its focus on one's eternal location of residence, here we find that salvation has more to do with our present and future immersion into heaven.

We are all walking along a path; at one end is hell and at the other end is heaven. The closer we get to either destination, the more similar to them we become, or the more immersed in them we become. As fallen humans, we are all naturally headed towards hell. We are facing hell and walking—if not running—towards it. Christ, however, made a way for us to turn around, to face heaven, and then walk—if not run—towards it.

I'm not speaking of heaven and hell as physical realms, but as descriptions of the fullness or void of God's presence. Heaven is heaven because God is there, and Hell is hell because God isn't there. And so, the more we run towards the presence of God, the more we need to throw off all the things that hold us back, slow us down, and pull us towards hell. The writer of the book of Hebrews tells us to run the race with endurance, throwing off all the sin that hinders (Hebrews 12:1–2). This is the point of salvation. It is to be free of sin, immersed in heaven, and transformed back into the image of God. It isn't a once and done idea.

Yes, salvation begins when we turn around and face heaven, but that's only the beginning. We face heaven so we can head that way, so we can walk that way, so we can be more like Jesus—who first laid the path we're walking, the path to godliness, Christlikeness, holiness, the image of God.

This reveals that Jesus didn't come just so we could know where we will spend eternity, but so we could change how we will spend it. He came so we could spend it as real, image-bearing humans, and not just broken and selfish creatures void of His presence and likeness.

Walls

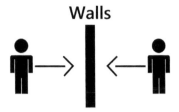

Freedom

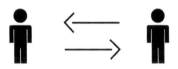

Exposed

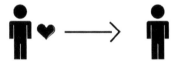

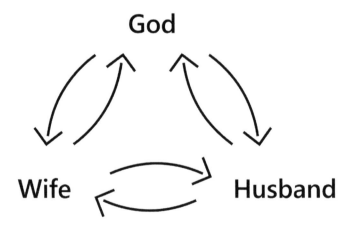

The first set of diagrams here reveals how our walls not only protect us, but also prevent the good we should be sharing from being shared. Once we lower the walls, we can actually give and receive—we can have relationships and communion. But a step beyond that isn't to just let down the walls, but to expose our hearts. If we want the love of God in our hearts to have an effect on others, then we need to give it in its most potent form, its raw form. To do that we need to make as direct a route as possible between our hearts and others; we need to expose our hearts to them, open and vulnerable.

This is risky business. Actually, it's so risky and vulnerable that the most intimate and vulnerable expression of this was reserved for the relationship between one man and one woman in marriage. The second diagram reveals how marriage was designed to reflect the image of God, probably more deeply and fully than any other relationship. It is in marriage that two people expose the most intimate and vulnerable aspects of their being to each other for the benefit of the other, and similarly do the same towards God. This becomes the model for family, and so for society, for community, and for world relations. If we lose the image of God in marriage, all of humanity suffers from that loss. Children need to be brought up witnessing this image in their families. It is there that they can learn and become reflections of the image of God as well. It is there that they see the picture of unity in diversity.

Marriage is the pinnacle, but all other relationships work similarly—just in different degrees and in different forms. But they all are based on the image of God, and how we need to remove the walls and expose our hearts to others in order to love them as God has loved us.

CHAPTER SIX

FLIMSY GOSPEL

I don't wish to make this chapter the primary thrust of this book, nor do I want it to be the foundation of what we discuss about the Gospel, for I fear that would become just another attempt to get away from our errors rather than actually being drawn to God. But I must express here why these diagrams and a fresh look at the Gospel are necessary.

I've spent my entire life in the Church. When I was baby, I went to church. When I was a teen, I went to Christian summer camp. When I was in my early twenties, I went to Bible college and began working as a pastor. There has never been a time in my life that I didn't regularly attend Sunday services, nor has there been a time when I seriously turned from the faith or rebelled against the establishment in some sort of burst of youthful freedom. I never rebelled as some teens and young adults do, but I did rebel in a different way.

I grew up in the Church, stayed in the Church, work in the Church (not necessarily for it), and am actually the first person in my family history to become a member of the clergy. I'm noting all this to say that in my own life, in my own church, and in the global Church as well—from North America all the way to the booming churches of China—we have some issues that need to be addressed. We've done something to the Gospel, and it's a problem that's been repeated throughout history. It's a problem that's crippling the true effectiveness of the Kingdom of God. We have made the Gospel into a flimsy, pathetic, cheap, easy, and dull story. And I'm at fault just as much as everyone else, if not more so than many.

When I was growing up, I was taught (and believed) that the Bible and God and all this stuff was true and accurate, and that if I wanted to go to heaven, I needed to ask Jesus into my heart. I had very little concept of what that meant, though I could remember the basic principles and language pretty well. I just knew that if I wanted the end goal of hell, I wouldn't ask Jesus into my heart, and if I wanted the end goal of eternal ice-cream sundaes, the hopes of a video game console in my bedroom, and potentially some stellar wings to fly around on in heaven, I'd better ask Jesus into my heart. And though my understanding of the theology surrounding all this developed further as I got older, it still remained essentially the same at the core: go to heaven, or go to hell.

Even when I had my encounter with love, the love of God, it was still in the context of the final goal. Nothing else really mattered, nor did anything else come much into play. When I started working at summer camp, we would talk to the kids about salvation and end up having a conversation about how they would start to want to do good things when they got saved, and would want to read their Bibles and pray. The formula was: get saved, want good things, do good things. The last two parts were just tacked on to the end, though.

It was all just a matter of making sure we got our ticket to heaven. Then once we had our ticket, we simply had to hold onto it. Life on earth was similar to wandering around an airport, checking out all the rare goodies at restaurants and souvenir shops while waiting to leave. There everything is overpriced and will most likely be confiscated by security or customs.

But something just didn't seem to fit. I began asking questions and looking deeper at these ideas, and problems began to surface. Eventually, chasms were revealed in the bedrock of this idea I had become so comfortable with and had proclaimed and defended for so long. That was when I began to see things differently, and when I decided to rebel. I decided to rebel against just accepting the ideas and teachings that had been presented and propagated for years. I decided to go back to the basics and see what it was all about for myself, from start to finish—to ask, "What's really the point of Christianity?"

I think the thing that threw me off the most was when I would have conversations with people who were supposed to know what they were doing, but seemed to be confused themselves. I remember having a talk with one evangelist about why it was necessary to evangelize if "God has already determined who would be saved and what is going to happen." His answer was less than satisfying, and so I began to look into that whole idea more. Then I started dating a girl who had very particular views on Bible versions and contemporary music, and had similar beliefs to this evangelist. In that new scenario, I found myself not just curious, but I was forced to start asking and searching out answers to these questions, to how this whole Christianity thing was supposed to work. Honestly, dating this girl made me question a lot of things—but that's a different story.

I spent time at Bible college reading books and attending classes. I found that the words I encountered were very poetic and usually accurate, but the explanation was still missing something. Everything I read and heard seemed to just come back to the Gospel being some kind of a weird situation caused by a divine being going about saving the world through arbitrary actions for reasons unknown and misunderstood. The images used were very epic and intense, but they just didn't seem to add up.

I would ask the question, "Couldn't God have saved the world without using Jesus?" and the answers would come back sporadic and vague, as if people were completely confident in their answers but had no idea what they were.

I would ask the question, "Does everything happen for a reason?" and the responses were unsurprising, but still unsettling when I looked at the environment of the world in which we all live.

I would ask, "If the purpose is to be saved, then why doesn't God take us to heaven immediately after we are saved, so as not to risk us falling away from Him?" and blank stares would form on the faces of those present, followed by the general cop-out answer, "God must have a reason."

Then there were the "if" statements—conditional promises found in the Old and New Testaments. Doctrines I was led to believe were universal seemed to have more wiggle room. Here are just a few of those statements (see the "Scripture References" list at the end of the book for more).

> *Now if you obey me fully and keep my covenant, then out of all nations you will be my treasured possession.*
> —Exodus 19:5, NIV

> *Now if you know these things, you will be blessed if you do them.*
> —John 13:17, NIV

These promises are conditional upon our actions or attitudes, and even our maintenance of those attitudes or actions.

When I look at the world, I have a hard time saying that everything happens for a reason, or that God has caused all things to happen. It doesn't make sense to me that God, who is incredibly practical and logical, would use an arbitrary method to fulfill some kind of legal obligation that has no foundation in the actual mechanics of the physical and spiritual world. I also find it confusing why, if the goal was only ever a destination (one which remained the same regardless of how much progress we made through the journey on earth), it required such complex and intense measures to bring about.

We say that God cannot have fellowship with sin, so He had to do something to get rid of the sin so we could be with Him—but why? Would it somehow taint His own being? Would it harm His reputation to be seen with sin? How would sacrifice clean up and remove sin and its consequences in the lives of sentient beings? These things just seemed to be missing pieces to me. Why did there seem to be so many gaps in the images and the processes? Was it just a matter of the mystery of salvation, or were we actually missing something that clarified those ideas?

Now, in reading back over this it sounds a bit like I don't even believe in the Gospel. I can feel myself asking: why does any of this matter? The whole thing does sound bad, and it does seem petty to be picking apart such a wonderful thing, but that's just it... it *does* sound bad! If I were to leave this message the way it has been presented to me, I would be left with something that lacks power and remains just a hopeful idea with little to do with my own life and being. To be told that once I get saved I will naturally want to do good things leaves an enormous hole. What if I *don't* naturally want to do good after I ask Jesus into my heart? What are these good things, and why would I want to do them? Does salvation have any effect on me, any purpose at all? Or is it just another arbitrary aspect of this process that is supposed to help me while I wait to go to heaven?

I actually find this very scary. We have made the gospel into a mystical idea that leaves us waiting to die. Even with much of the now popular writing concerning social action and living out our faith in our everyday lives, we are still just waiting to die. We want heaven, and we want others to go there too, so we all end up waiting to die together.

When we do some digging, we find that this idea is actually rooted in the philosophy of Plato and the heretical teaching of Gnosticism. Though masked by poetry and good intentions, this teaching makes the present physical world out to be something less valuable than the future spiritual world. It makes this present life worthless, and leads to the idea that our money, our bodies, our neighbours, and our world don't intrinsically have value, because they are just shadows. We are to care for them simply as a test of our will, and as discipline in our growth. Yet, the last time I checked, Plato was a pagan rather than a Christian, and Gnosticism is heretical (meaning that it is contrary to Scripture, and has been condemned by the Church for the past two thousand years).

The Gospel has been turned into a kind of vertical escapism. This often manifests itself as legalism. Either we are extremely strict and must follow all the rules set down for us so that we won't lose our place in heaven, or we hold to the idea that once we ask Jesus into our hearts, nothing can take our place in heaven from us because it's now our legal right. This is best seen in the diagram from Chapter Five where there is a line between hell and heaven and we must cross it. The entire focus is to be on the heaven side, safe and sound. But this is an incredibly flimsy gospel. It is a gospel concerned solely with the vertical aspect of reality (you and God).

Why flimsy? Because it is thin, easily manipulated, doesn't hold up against pressure, and doesn't have the strength to make changes. It focuses on something so distant that the only reason to change now is to maintain our status. It only requires anything of us so that we can get something in return, and thus we will only ever go as far as we have to, never the extra mile. It is based on devaluing the present and the physical, as if they are somehow less important or less eternal than anything else. It functions on the assumption that the here and now are doomed, that this world and this time are just sticking around to get destroyed, that evil has won and we need to get our escape route planned.

It assumes that God is so small and so impotent that He cannot actually save this world, save this time, or do anything worthwhile now, and has to fall back to some kind of a strategic secondary location. It assumes that the Holy Spirit exists only to... well, honestly, with this model I'm not even sure if the Holy Spirit exists for anything. He may convict someone to come to be saved, and He may hint towards things to do, but He is nothing more than a glorified angel on the shoulder with less power than Satan.

Does this sound anything like the God we have discussed? Does this sound anything like the God of the Exodus, the God who took the evil of the Israelites being enslaved and used it to reveal His power to the entire world? The God who stood against every known power and resource and conquered them? The God who made it clear that anything outside the truth has no value, because He is the truth?

No. A powerful God like that wouldn't be bound by such a weak and distant model—one powerless to change anything except one's future destination. What happened to the God that changes things in the present?

This is the question my generation and I are asking, and throughout history there is a phenomenon that can be likened to a pendulum. From generation to generation, there is typically a shift in philosophy. On one side is legalism, where my parent's generation found themselves. Then on the other side is something called humanism, where my generation is headed. Like a pendulum, we swing from one extreme to the other: legalism to humanism and back. One generation sees the errors of one extreme and attempts to correct it so violently that they swing past the truth and end up with another extreme. Then the next generation sees the errors of that extreme and attempts to correct it so violently that they swing past the truth again and end up back at the first extreme. Back and forth we go.

My generation sees how escapism leaves our world and its people out in the cold, and so we push for social justice and human rights. We look at our neighbours and are so overwhelmed for them that we pick up every cause we can think of and start rioting, petitioning, and campaigning. We see how people are treated, and we fight for them. We fight for them so hard that we think we can actually save the world and fix everything. We think we are the salvation of the world, and God and heaven and forgiveness are just good ideas designed to motivate us to be better neighbours. We become so convinced of our own potential that we take good things like human rights, the economy, and the care of the planet and push them to extremes, hoping the extreme will finally produce change.

We fight for people's rights: rights to suicide, rights to abortion, rights to sexual expression, rights to never be offended, rights to say whatever we want, even before we ask if those rights are essential or even good. We begin to assume that money and wealth can solve problems, even though the rich and famous suffer from depression just as frequently as anyone else. We demand tolerance by spewing hatred. We fight for the environment and wildlife until we come to the conclusion that if we were to sacrifice humanity entirely, Mother Nature would finally have the offering she requires. Or we just let everyone do whatever they want, then realize too late that people can't coexist like that without coming to hate each other. In our attempt to save the world, we give saltwater to a people dying of thirst.

So back and forth we swing.

Generation to generation we swing.

Humanism to legalism to humanism to legalism.

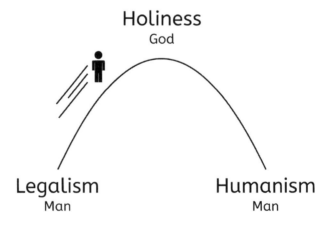

And humanism has the same flimsy qualities that legalism does. It denies God's truth, allowing mankind to determine what is right and wrong. It denies God's ability to define what is right and thus to reveal what is wrong. It says that all religions have the same principles, pointing towards what God wants us to do, but ignoring the statement of the Exodus. It denies the necessity of the Holy Spirit to change anything, because "Man can do it all on his own." It makes discipleship, and the work we do to help others, into something shallow and meaningless because it is so concerned with the present that it forgets that there is a future that must be dealt with as well. It works in the here and now to such an extent that it builds up a kind of treasure that will soon fade away, because no matter what we do, we will all die. *Our* world, *our* rules, *our* plans, *our* power—and we deny God's ability to do anything; He is far off and distant. Humanity develops some kind of horizontal messianic complex. It is a Gospel concerned solely with the horizontal (you and me).

Incredibly, this is essentially the same thing as legalism, just in a different form. Both place the power and control in the hands of humanity. One controls their eternity by the rules they follow and the things they believe. The other controls their world by their actions and ideas. They are the centre of their worlds, and God is powerless to do anything beyond them. They both assume that God is powerless to touch the physical lives of people, to deal with health issues, financial problems, global poverty, greed, war, politics, temptation, sin, the internet, technology, film, our governments, philosophies, religions, the environment, weather, family, sex, and everything else.

One generation will hold strongly to this idea of a dual reality where the spiritual is at war with the physical. It may not say that explicitly, but that is what its actions and values portray. It is the hope for a set apart life where one waits until death to find what is really valuable. It places the worth of people and the world only in the spiritual that will endure past the judgment, and that is the sole time we will find worth or value or freedom. Then another generation will rise up and fight for the people, seeking to free them from tyranny and oppression. They will look to the rights of the people and make sure that everyone is treated equally and with respect, never with judgment.

Reading back over that paragraph, I almost have trouble seeing what is wrong with either picture. They both emphasize some compelling and appealing ideals. That is, until I remember how one focus results in the neglect of the other. It is very rare to see the Gospel expressed in a way that acknowledges the holiness of God and uses that fact as the basis for how we must fight for others in the present.

With the vertical gospel we end up leaving our world out in the cold.

With the horizontal gospel we end up bringing a blanket to the starving.

We either don't care to change the world, or we are powerless to do it.

We either vainly attempt to reach God, or we think we already have.

We see problems with where we are, and in an attempt to run away from it we overshoot where we should be. Though we find holiness for a while, we inevitably overshoot the target and find ourselves on the other side of the spiritual mountain. The goal cannot be to fix the past generation's failures. God must pull us up to the top, like a person pulling another up with a rope. The rope draws us in and holds us at the top. God must be the centre and the source. So, maybe we need to stop running from where we are, and begin to run towards where we should be.

Maybe what we need is a gospel that combines the vertical and the horizontal aspects of these two ideas, one that brings the holiness of God to the people *and* changes things. One that calls people out and doesn't leave them where they are, but goes to them and shows them life beyond just the hope of death. A Christian isn't someone who believes in Jesus, or someone who likes His philosophies, but someone that is actually like Him.

What if we stopped with this hopeless flimsy gospel and looked for a Gospel that had both the vertical and the horizontal? What if we looked for a Gospel that was based on God and not us? What if the Gospel we need—the Gospel of the Bible—was more than just heaven or earth? What if God was allowed to be the centre, the beginning, and the end? What if the Gospel was about God bringing heaven to the Earth by restoring a design based on Himself, manifested and returned to humanity through Jesus, spread through human relationships with each other and God by the Holy Spirit?

1 Peter 2:9 (ESV) says,

But you are a chosen race, a royal priesthood, a holy nation, a people for his own possession, that you may proclaim the excellencies of him who called you out of darkness into his marvelous light.

What if the Gospel was more like this?
I believe it is, and this is where we now turn.

CHAPTER SEVEN

THE LAW AND PROPHETS

L eaving behind the flimsy gospel, we now turn to the heart of the Gospel of Jesus Christ. This isn't just good news found in the New Testament, as if the Old Testament was a failed attempt to fix the problem. This Gospel isn't a swing from one idea to another, but the culmination of thousands of years of work and preparation. And if we pay attention, we will find that the heart of the Gospel is even apparent in the Law and the Prophets.

> And [Jesus] said to him, "You shall love the Lord your God with all your heart and with all your soul and with all your mind. This is the great and first commandment. And a second is like it; You shall love your neighbor as yourself. On these two commandments depend all the Law and the Prophets."
> —Matthew 22:37–40, ESV

The Law was given to the Israelites after they were freed from Egypt in the Exodus, and it was God's guide to how they were supposed to live. There are some strange things contained in the Law that don't make sense to us today, but would have been very clear and important to the people of that time. There are sacrifices that really did nothing themselves for the people other than give them a way to show they trusted God. The sacrifices also were put in place to look forward to when God would sacrifice something huge in order to actually heal the people. There are principles of community and cleanliness that expressed the foundation of a healthy society. Yet some people look at the law and see just a bunch of legalistic rules, missing the motive and heart in them that is vital to all life. The Law established an explicit guide for living in two key relationships: relationship with God and relationship with each other.

There is a summary statement in the Law that says:

Love the Lord your God with all your heart and with all your soul and with all your strength.
—Deuteronomy 6:5, NIV

Then there are the well-known Ten Commandments:

You shall have no other gods before me.

You shall not make for yourself an image in the form of anything in heaven above or on the earth beneath or in the waters below…

You shall not misuse the name of the Lord your God, for the Lord will not hold anyone guiltless who misuses his name.

Observe the Sabbath day by keeping it holy, as the Lord your God has commanded you…

Honor your father and your mother, as the Lord your God has commanded you, so that you may live long and that it may go well with you in the land the Lord your God is giving you.

You shall not murder.

You shall not commit adultery.

You shall not steal.

You shall not give false testimony against your neighbor.

You shall not covet your neighbor's wife...

—Deuteronomy 5:7–21, NIV

These ten commandments can be split into two parts. Commandments one through four concern our relationship with God, and commandments five through ten concern our relationships with each other. If we read through the rest of the Law, we will see that God gave His people very specific guidelines and ways to maintain the relationships they were designed for.

Even as we study and examine the Law in the book of Leviticus, we will find that there is a common focus on one's relationship with God and one's relationship with other humans. The relationship with God is a vertical dynamic, and the relationship with other humans is a horizontal dynamic. Here are a few examples of laws concerning the horizontal relationship:

You shall not take vengeance or bear a grudge against the sons of your own people, but you shall love your neighbor as yourself: I am the Lord.

—Leviticus 19:18, ESV

When a stranger sojourns with you in your land, you shall not do him wrong. You shall treat the stranger who sojourns with you as the native among you, and you shall love him as yourself, for you were strangers in the land of Egypt: I am the Lord your God.

—Leviticus 19:33–34, ESV

If your brother becomes poor and cannot maintain himself with you, you shall support him as though he were a stranger and a sojourner, and he shall live with you. Take no interest from him or profit, but fear your God, that

*your brother may live beside you. You shall not lend him
your money at interest, nor give him your food for profit.*
—Leviticus 25:35–37, ESV

The Law concerning one's horizontal relationships has an intrinsic connection to the Law concerning one's relationship with God. The avoidance or disobedience of either the horizontal or vertical would result in a failure to fulfill the other. If people ignore God, they will start hurting each other. If they ignore each other, they will start betraying God. This dynamic is important to keep in mind, and will come up again later.

But the guidance of the Law wasn't enough. After the Law was given and the Israelites finally settled in the Promised Land, just like every other human civilization and every other human person, they began to forget who they were. They forgot that God was God and they were not. They forgot that they had been made in His image to be like Him, and so refused the clear direction God gave them and decided to do things their own way.

The time of the Judges is a horrifying display of where this leads. The Israelites ended up fighting, raping, killing, using, and abusing each other, and defiling their relationships with others and with God. By the end of the book, we think we are reading something from an R-rated slasher movie. Because of this terrible situation, God eventually sent men and women to try to get the Israelites back on track. They had gone awry, and instead of just abandoning them, like we typically do with our crazy relatives, God sent them the prophets.

There are many prophets of God, and many of them have their own books in the Bible. It is in these books that we can see the heart of God cry out to the people, to humanity, about what He wants for them. They also show us just how we have so terribly messed everything up.

For example, the prophet Hosea literally lived out an illustration of how God feels about our situation. God told Hosea to marry a prostitute. Then He told him that when she ran off to all her clients, he was to buy her back and not let her go any more. This was to give the Israelites a physical example of how they had run around with every god, idea, theory, object, relationship, idol, power, and lust under the sun, even after they had devoted themselves to God alone. The Israelites ran around with anything that would have them. God used the life of Hosea to show that He would still be willing to buy them back. The door was still open. He would bring them home, not so they could continue their old ways, but so He could give them real life and meaning—a safe, committed, fulfilling relationship.

Another book tells the story of the prophet Jeremiah, which we have examined in part already. Jeremiah looked toward a time when we would have new hearts, when we wouldn't need to keep track of all the rules and guidelines because we would be reprogrammed from the inside out. Jeremiah was a man overwhelmed by the presence and Word of God; he suffered throughout his life for the stand he took, and yet called the people out on their idolatry, their wickedness, and their evil. Even when they were headed to exile, he gave them hope of how God would still be fighting for them. God gave them every opportunity to come back to Him, but He knew many would not. They would continue to live lives of selfishness and evil, they would be punished for their pride and hatred, and they would be removed from creation.

There is also the story of Ezekiel, who dreamed of heaven and the future glory God would bring. He dreamed of a valley full of such death that the bodies were not just corpses, not just raw skeletons, but dry bones with no life left in them at all. Yet, in his dream he saw God bring life to even this valley that was seemingly, logically, beyond hope. He proclaimed a message of God's desire and ability to remove the cold dead heart of even the most far gone and give them life, repair all damage, free every bond, defeat even the most hopeless situations, and give them a brand new, pure heart. Ezekiel also shared a word from God about how far gone the world had become and how upsetting the behaviour of humanity was. This is what he said:

God's Message came to me: "Son of man, prophesy against
the shepherd-leaders of Israel. Yes, prophesy! Tell those
shepherds, 'God, the Master, says: Doom to you shepherds
of Israel, feeding your own mouths! Aren't shepherds sup-
posed to feed sheep? You drink the milk, you make clothes
from the wool, you roast the lambs, but you don't feed the
sheep. You don't build up the weak ones, don't heal the
sick, don't doctor the injured, don't go after the strays,
don't look for the lost. You bully and badger them. And
now they're scattered every which way because there was
no shepherd—scattered and easy pickings for wolves and
coyotes. Scattered—my sheep!—exposed and vulnerable
across mountains and hills. My sheep scattered all over
the world, and no one out looking for them!
　　　　　—Ezekiel 34:1–6, MSG (emphasis in original)

Then there is the story of Isaiah, who had a vision of God in
the Temple, a vision where the angels surrounded God singing
"Holy, Holy, Holy." This man, this prophet, fell in fear and humil-
iation for seeing the greatness of God, and thus recognizing his
own insignificance. It was in this humility that God called Him
and showed him incredible things about the true nature of heav-
en and earth, the law, and what they were intended to do. Isaiah
proclaimed a life not filled with empty religious acts, but acts that
flowed from a heart overwhelmed with adoration for God and
love for his neighbour.

But Isaiah also shared a word from God concerning how the
people had continued with their religious traditions in a way that
had corrupted them into a sort of karma system—they thought
they would get good things if they did good things. It corrupted
God's call on them into a manipulating and self-serving religion,
rather than the self-sacrificing model of God's character. This is
what he said:

Shout! A full-throated shout!
> *Hold nothing back—a trumpet-blast shout!*
> *Tell my people what's wrong with their lives,*
> *face my family Jacob with their sins!*
> *They're busy, busy, busy at worship,*
> *and love studying all about me.*
> *To all appearances they're a nation of right-living*
people—
> *law-abiding, God-honoring.*
> *They ask me, "What's the right thing to do?"*
> *and love having me on their side.*
> *But they also complain,*
> *"Why do we fast and you don't look our way?*
> *Why do we humble ourselves and you don't even no-*
tice?"
> *Well, here's why:*
> *The bottom line on your "fast days" is profit.*
> *You drive your employees much too hard.*
> *You fast, but at the same time you bicker and fight.*
> *You fast, but you swing a mean fist.*
> *The kind of fasting you do*
> *won't get your prayers off the ground.*
> *Do you think this is the kind of fast day I'm after:*
> *a day to show off humility?*
> *To put on a pious long face*
> *and parade around solemnly in black?*
> *Do you call that fasting,*
> *a fast day that I, God, would like?*
> *This is the kind of fast day I'm after:*
> *to break the chains of injustice,*
> *get rid of exploitation in the workplace,*
> *free the oppressed,*
> *cancel debts.*
> *What I'm interested in seeing you do is:*
> *sharing your food with the hungry,*

inviting the homeless poor into your homes,
putting clothes on the shivering ill-clad,
being available to your own families.
Do this and the lights will turn on,
and your lives will turn around at once.
Your righteousness will pave your way.
The God of glory will secure your passage.
Then when you pray, God will answer.
You'll call out for help and I'll say, 'Here I am.'
— Isaiah 58:1–9, MSG (emphasis in the original—
read the whole chapter on your own for more)

There is the story of Micah, who shared with the people that God did not require sacrifices from them, and they could not control Him with their sacrifices. Micah made it clear that what God desired more than sacrifices was for people to live the way they were designed to, not the way they had chosen to. God used Micah to call out the people and show them how they had forgotten the heart of the Law—how they had ignored its purpose and forgotten to maintain the right horizontal relationships, and so had also neglected their vertical relationship.

But he's already made it plain how to live, what to do,
   what God is looking for in men and women.
   It's quite simple: Do what is fair and just to your
neighbor,
   be compassionate and loyal in your love,
   And don't take yourself too seriously—
   take God seriously.
                                      — Micah 6:8, MSG

Then I said:
   "Listen, leaders of Jacob, leaders of Israel:
   Don't you know anything of justice?
   Haters of good, lovers of evil:

Isn't justice in your job description?
But you skin my people alive.
You rip the meat off their bones.
You break up the bones, chop the meat,
and throw it in a pot for cannibal stew."
The time's coming, though, when these same leaders
will cry out for help to God, but he won't listen.
He'll turn his face the other way
because of their history of evil.
Here is God's Message to the prophets,
the preachers who lie to my people:
"For as long as they're well paid and well fed,
the prophets preach, 'Isn't life wonderful! Peace to all!'
But if you don't pay up and jump on their bandwagon,
their 'God bless you' turns into 'God damn you.'
Therefore, you're going blind. You'll see nothing.
You'll live in deep shadows and know nothing.
The sun has set on the prophets.
They've had their day; from now on it's night.
Visionaries will be confused,
experts will be all mixed up.
They'll hide behind their reputations and make
lame excuses to cover up their God-ignorance."
—Micah 3:1–7, MSG

Then there is the last prophet of the Old Testament, Malachi, who looked forward to the coming of a man who would prepare the way of the one who would make everything new. He looked forward, four hundred years before it happened, to the time when a man would come like the old prophet Elijah. He looked forward to a man we know as John the Baptist, who got people thinking and looking for the one who would save them (Malachi 4:5).

And four hundred years later, the one who would save them actually came...

Jesus was born of a virgin in the town of Bethlehem. It was here that God became a man—sinless, perfect, humble. He went from the glory of the almighty, all-powerful God of the universe, and became a lowly, fragile human being. He came just as we all have, through birth from a woman. He grew up as we have, but lived differently than we did. And while on the earth Jesus said incredible things, did incredible things, and also said something that no one else could have said: *"I am the way and the truth and the life"* (John 14:6, NIV).

This statement holds remarkable meaning for us today, and it was one of many things Jesus said and did that made Him the enemy of anyone who sought to exploit and use others. Unlike the Law, which could be twisted and manipulated, Jesus was steadfast. He was life, and those that didn't like that idea hated Him for it.

Eventually, Jesus was captured and put on display for everyone to watch as He was tortured and killed. They stretched His arms out wide and nailed them in place, and waited for Him to die. Then after he died, they took His body and set it in a tomb. That was Friday, and then on Sunday, the third day, He came back to life. After reconnecting with His disciples, Jesus ascended to heaven and sent us the Holy Spirit, which is the setting in which we still find ourselves today.

It's important to understand that the Law, in itself, is not what Jesus was trying to live up to. The Law was not, and is not, the be all and end all. The Law was put in place as a shadow of Jesus, a preparation for Jesus—not a requirement for Jesus to fulfill. He didn't come to be the sacrifice that the Law demanded. No, the Law mandated sacrifices in order to prepare people for the sacrifice Jesus would make. The Law is subject to Jesus, not vice versa. But the Law isn't bad either. The Law reflected Jesus, looked forward to Him, pointed those who were paying attention in the right direction, and expressed the heart of God. In Jesus, the heart of God was brought back to humanity, just as the prophets had prophesied: hope was realized and things could now really change.

If we look at the Law and Prophets, the story of the Gospel, the story of Jesus, we learn several things:

The first thing we learn is that God initiates the act of redemption out of His own will and desire, not out of our actions or because we deserve it or because we do something that makes Him happy. When we are in the thick of evil, He chooses to love us. So, as we have seen already: love is unconditional, but relationship isn't.

God always presents the option, always takes the first step, always shows grace, always loves before any good of man. Yet, it's clear that when that love isn't reciprocated there is a break in the relationship, and relationship is the essence of life. Adam and Eve reject God, the relationship breaks, their image is broken, and the world is cursed because they have pushed God away. Israel rejects God, the relationship breaks and their fate becomes uncertain, some are doomed and swallowed by the earth, others are bitten by snakes, and some of them fall into a condition where they kill each other. They lack the love that sustains life because they rejected Him and set their own fate.

God gives guidelines and laws, but if we choose to reject them, we reject Him, resulting in His love and life not being in us. How can we have the image of life—the image of God—if we reject God, and if we reject the image of life? To reject life is to embrace death. It may not be a quick, simple death, but a spiritual, mental, and physical death that takes years. Our minds, souls, and bodies will be corrupted, and slowly draw us into the darkness. Only in a relationship with God, which is conditional upon accepting a love that doesn't sit idly by, will we find life.

The Law and Prophets show us that at the core of this love relationship is the restoration of the image of God. By "image," I refer less to a physical visage and more to a relational dynamic. This Gospel is a restoration of the vertical and horizontal relationships. This is why Jesus summed everything up into the two great commands: to love God above all else, and love your neighbour as yourself (Matthew 22:37–40).

Throughout the Law, we see statements concerning how we relate to God and how we relate to each other. As we've seen in Chapter Five, our vertical and horizontal relationships reflect the inner dynamics of the Trinity. Yet when there is a breach in either the vertical or the horizontal, we cease to reflect the image of God. The vertical, our connection with God, and the horizontal, our connection with each other, must both be intact and functioning properly if we are to be the image of God. We only look like true humans when we love God and we love others the right way.

We cannot properly love horizontally unless we have the vertical love. Likewise, we cannot properly love vertically unless we have the horizontal love. When I refer to love from here on out, I mean true *agape* love, not a cheap or tainted love. When I say we must love each other, I mean we must serve others without the thought of getting something back in any way, shape, or form. Thus, we show our love for God by how we treat each other, and we love each other when we are loving God. What could make God happier than to see His people living the way they were designed to? What could change the world more than when people love God with everything they are?

It cannot be one or the other: it must be both. This is what the entire Old Testament speaks to. The power of this calling was brought back to humanity through the returning of the image of God Himself in Jesus. No arbitrary action or thought could make humans do what they were supposed to, and no random idea would fix the damage to humanity. The goal was never just to save sinners so they could live forever in their broken way—it was always that they wouldn't be broken anymore! This wasn't only the goal, but the solution.

What better way to restore this vertical and horizontal design in the world than for Jesus to come and begin restoring the design through His own human life, which would then begin restoring the design in the lives of those He built relationships with?

And then they, in turn, would restore the design in the lives of those around them as they began to live it. They were restoring the image of God to humanity by living as the image of God.

Nothing else could have done this. Why don't we just die after we are saved? Why did Jesus have to come as He did? Because the goal was never just individuals without sin: the goal was humanity living as the image of God. This is only accomplished and spread through what Jesus did, and by what He called us to: making disciples.

It was never about crossing a line of commitment; it was about turning from the direction we were headed—the direction of deception and selfishness—to the direction of godliness (like-god-ness, not being our own gods) and becoming who we were made to be. It was never about a place; it was about being fixed, repaired, restored, regenerated (notice the "re-" words, which show a return to a previous state, one we were designed for at the beginning), and made new.

This is both a crisis in turning and a process in growth. It is both repentance and obedience. Getting saved and then getting discipled aren't separate things—they are two parts of the same process, being remade in the image of God. Sanctification (becoming holy, to reflect God) is the point; salvation is just the start of the process of changing our entire lives from the inside out to become like Jesus. This is the plot we had misplaced.

From the very beginning of Creation, throughout the Biblical text from Old Testament to New Testament, God has been pointing everything back towards His own image. Everything has been pointing towards His image returning to humanity, manifested first in Adam and Eve and then restored in Jesus. Everything can be summed up by two commands, illustrated and affirmed in the Old Testament Law and Prophets and then made real in Jesus Christ. It all comes back to His image.

God brought His own image back to His creatures by becoming one of those creatures. When we look at Jesus, we see what we were designed to be. We see a human being loving God and loving others, just as the Father loves the Spirit and the Spirit loves the Father, the Father the Son and the Son the Father, the Spirit the Son and the Son the Spirit.

In this vertical and horizontal expression, we begin to see the broken become new. It is almost like we are given a fresh start... born again even... (see John 3).

Jesus is what makes heaven heavenly. He is the goal—to know Him more, to be like Him more, to have Him live in us more is heaven... and it starts now. This is the Way, the Truth and the Life of the gospel.

> *I am the way and the truth and the life. No one comes to the Father except through me.*
>
> —Jesus, speaking in John 14:6, NIV

CHAPTER EIGHT

THE REVERSAL

"I can't believe in God because there's too much evil in the world!"

Maybe you've said that before, or maybe you've heard someone else say it. One way or another, we're all familiar with this statement. It assumes God can't or won't do anything about evil.

But everything we know about God shows us something different.

It has become popular in contemporary western Christianity to focus entirely on the New Testament, as if the Gospel was only developed and expressed when Jesus came to the earth as a man. As we saw in the previous chapter, elements of God's grace and work have been apparent since the time of the Law and the Prophets. They pointed to the coming of Christ from the beginning, and when He came He fulfilled the prophecies and the Law.

But there's another aspect to this that we need to examine carefully: the reversal. It is knowing and trusting in God's ability to change things, fix things, reach people, and take even the most terrible person and situations of this life and redeem them.

This has been the plan ever since humanity fell from the glory of God. (I'm going to be skipping a lot of details for the sake of time and space. Besides that, I don't tell the story as well as the Bible does, so you should probably read Genesis on your own when you get the chance.)

God created the universe out of nothing. He is the only being able to do that. Humans can only imagine things; they don't actually create from nothing. Our imaginations often just take ideas and mix them about. Rarely, if ever, do people have a purely original thought.

When God finished creating the world, He made Adam in His own image. But there was a problem with this human: there was only one of him. In the entire creation account, this is the only time God says that something isn't good. He looks at the man He has created and says, *"It is not good for the man to be alone"* (Genesis 2:18, NIV). God then proceeds to create the complement to the man—the woman.

Humanity now had male and female. The female came from the male, and all other males would come from the females (1 Corinthians 11:12). The sexes were completely dependent on each other, but at the same time independent of each other. Man was no longer alone, and it was good.

God then gave humanity a command: to care for the earth and to be fruitful and multiply. They were in perfect relationship with each other and with God. They knew nothing other than the love that had created them. They had been created to love God, to love each other, and to spread that love beyond themselves.

But love is always a choice, so God presented humanity with a choice. He put a tree on the earth and instructed humanity not to eat its fruit, because they would die if they did. They then had to choose whether to love like God or to go their own way and eat the forbidden fruit. Whatever happened next would be the result of free will, not mindless puppetry or programming. Obedience would be love, and disobedience would be rejection.

This is where our story gets messy—yes, *our* story—and where we first catch a glimpse of the Gospel.

Even if you've never heard this story, you can figure out what happened. Adam and Eve, the first humans, made in the image of God, ate fruit from the tree they weren't supposed to eat from. When they did this, they noticed that they were naked. They were ashamed of their nakedness and knew good and evil.

I don't think there was anything special in the fruit of that tree, which happened to be called the Tree of Knowledge of Good and Evil. No, I think the act of disobedience was what opened their eyes to the world they later wished they had never known. By rejecting the command of God, they had acted evilly, and so knew evil and became evil.

Designed for selfless love, they now came to seek after power and knowledge. In rejecting who they were, they aspired to be something they were not, and so ceased to be who they'd been created to be. In disobeying God, they ceased to be living physical expressions of *agape*.

They ceased to do everything they had been designed for. They ceased to be the image of God. They stopped being with God, and so they were cut off from the source of their identity. They attempted to remove themselves from the triune relationship and consequently ran straight into the loneliness of selfishness.

Adam and Eve turned on each other almost immediately, and the world was changed. This was the first death.

The Bible says that God cursed the world, I think to reflect humanity's new nature. We chose to be selfish rather than selfless, and the world reflected that. Pain in childbirth, our limited time on earth, bad weather, pain in work, fragile and frail bodies, and a selfish and dangerous world of beasts and environments all reflected our broken nature.

Because of our actions, the world we were commanded to care for was cursed to reflect us. The creatures God had designed to be the guardians of His creation, the shining beacon of His character and image, did the opposite of what they were made for. Even a short look at recorded history reveals just how broken the world is—and we caused that brokenness.

God had every right to remove humanity from his creation. We're like a washing machine that's designed to clean clothes, but just makes them dirtier. Or a GPS designed to get us to our destination, but that always takes us in the wrong direction. We were designed for one thing, but did the opposite. It's like hiring somebody to watch and protect our kids, only to come home to them playing with knives, watching adult videos, and having been abused. Any such person we hired wouldn't be kept around, and would have to face some serious consequences. But God doesn't simply punish or destroy; He begins a work that will change everything.

God said this: *"I will put enmity between you [Satan] and the woman, and between your offspring and her offspring; he shall bruise your head, and you shall bruise his heel"* (Genesis 3:15, ESV).

This is absolutely vital to understanding everything else in the Bible. This is the promise of the Gospel.

When Adam and Eve were at the Tree of Knowledge of Good and Evil, Satan, the great deceiver, was there. Satan tempted them, and they gave in. He didn't make the choice for them, but he did tempt them, and God makes the above statement about him. I believe this to be a promise fulfilled in Jesus. I believe this statement was a promise to the deceiver—to deception, to illusion, to lies, to evil—that one day Jesus would come and utterly crush him. I also believe this to be a promise that is continually expressed in the Old Testament. God takes evil and turns it around to create good.

Moving through the book of Genesis, we see humanity becoming increasingly corrupt, destroying the land and becoming violent towards each other. Their sense of right and wrong became more and more skewed, to the point that they thought evil was good. It would have been as if everyone in the world shared the hatefulness and arrogance of Hitler, the KKK, ISIS, President Snow, Voldemort, Darth Sidious, Kahn, Bane, General Zod, or Scar.

God was disgusted with how they had betrayed their calling and gone completely against the purpose of creation. He determined the best thing to do was to destroy everything through a flood and start over, so He set a plan in motion to flood the world and wipe it clean. But there was one man—Noah—who honoured God. God saw his life and called him to build a boat to save his family and enough animals to start over after the flood. Even with God's right to wipe the world clean, He made space to fix rather than destroy. After the flood, God put a sign in the sky, a rainbow, to signify that He would never again take such extreme measures as to flood the whole world.

We would have destroyed ourselves and our world, but we were given another chance. God took evil and turned it around to create good. Yet, humanity slipped back into its old habits, and the world became corrupt and evil once again.

As you follow the story of Genesis, you will eventually encounter a man named Abraham who decides to follow God even though he has no idea where God is leading him. This is what God says to him in Genesis 12:1–3 (ESV):

Go from your country and your kindred and your father's house to the land that I will show you. And I will make of you a great nation, and I will bless you and make your name great, so that you will be a blessing. I will bless those who bless you, and him who dishonors you I will curse, and in you all the families of the earth shall be blessed.

God told Abraham that He was going to bless him in order to bless others—so that the whole world would be blessed. With no specific details on how, or when, or where, God called Abraham to trust Him so He could use him to bless the entire world. This wasn't something new. This wasn't a different promise or act than what God had said in the garden; it was a confirmation. He was beginning to flesh out how He would crush evil. He would use His people (those who trust Him) to change the world!

As we read the Old Testament, we begin to see this promise come about. The whole world was to be blessed through those who followed Abraham's example and trusted God. This became apparent in the life of a man named Joseph.

Joseph was a descendant of Abraham, and had ten older brothers. These brothers were jealous of him to the point that they wanted to kill him. Their father loved Joseph more than the rest of them, and they hated Joseph for it. Eventually, they trapped Joseph and considered killing him, but instead faked his death and sold him into slavery. Joseph remained faithful to God, though, and despite the evil, God determined He would turn it around to do something good.

Joseph ended up becoming a slave in Egypt. Then, through a series of rather disheartening events where he consistently did the right things and got punished for them, he eventually found himself speaking with Pharaoh. In this conversation, Joseph's obedience to God, and dependence on Him, paid off. Pharaoh asked Joseph to interpret a dream, and Joseph was able to. Because Joseph sought God's knowledge and knew God's voice, he was able to reveal the truth contained in the dream.

Joseph pointed not to his own abilities, but to God's ability to interpret dreams; he was just the messenger. Pharaoh was still impressed, though. He made Joseph second-in-command for the entire country! The dream had been about an approaching famine, and Pharaoh knew he needed someone wise to prepare for it. Joseph was that someone.

The famine eventually got so bad that Joseph's brothers began to feel the effects in their homeland and had to travel to Egypt to find food. When they showed up in Egypt, Joseph recognized them, but they didn't recognize him. And again, through a series of incredible events, Joseph discovered that they were sorry for what they had done to him, and he finally revealed who he was. Joseph then invited them to stay with him in Egypt. But, naturally, after what they had done, his brothers were nervous. They thought that Joseph was just biding his time until he could exact his revenge on them, but this is what Joseph then said to them:

Do not fear, for am I in the place of God? As for you, you meant evil against me, but God meant it for good, to bring about that many people should be kept alive, as they are today.

—Genesis 50:19–20, ESV

Joseph's brothers intended to get rid of him because they hated him, but God used their plot to bring about good. Because Joseph was sold into slavery, he was eventually put in a position to prepare the known world for a terrible famine and save them. God used an act intended for evil to bring about good. It's like God had somehow reversed the curse and turned it into a blessing. This was a sign of God fulfilling His promise to Abraham, and a foreshadowing of what would come. A curse had been turned into a blessing for the entire known world. When everyone in Egypt and the surrounding countries would have died from famine, they were saved because God reversed a curse. As with the promise to Adam and Eve, and His work with Noah, there had been some awful consequences to humanity's evil, but God was turning it back on itself to bring about good instead.

We see this same thing happen over and over again.

There was the time when a man named Judah ignored his daughter-in-law, and then slept with her because he thought she was a prostitute. Judah ended up being shown how selfish he was, but also gained a son who would continue his family line all the way to Jesus.

There was the time when the Israelites were freed from Egypt after they had been slaves for four hundred years, and then disobeyed God and ended up wandering in the desert for forty years. But during that time, God was able to teach them what it means to trust Him.

Then there is King David. Though said to have been a man after God's own heart, David had his weaknesses, and he eventually gave in to them. He was on his balcony one night looking out over the city and saw a naked woman—Bathsheba—washing herself, and David lost his head. He called his servants and told them to bring her to him. After he had his way with her, David sent her home. She later sent him word to let him know that he had gotten her pregnant—this wasn't just a problem because it was a one-night-stand, but because she was already married to one of David's most celebrated soldiers, one who happened to be at war for David. You can read the full story in 2 Samuel 11.

David panicked, and through a series of desperate attempts to cover his tracks, eventually had Bathsheba's husband killed and took her as his new wife. But the consequences continued. Bathsheba's child died soon after he was born, and David had some extreme family conflicts over the next few years, leaving him ashamed and his family disgraced. It seemed like this failure had a never-ending series of negative effects. This evil was destroying David's family and the entire nation with it—but God was able to use it anyway.

David had another son, Solomon, with Bathsheba, and he became the next king. He was one of the wisest men who had ever lived, wrote the Old Testament book of Ecclesiastes and parts of the Proverbs, and gained world renown for his insights. He still had some significant faults, like his father, but God brought good out of an act of evil. Despite the negative consequences and loss, God was able to make something good out of something awful.

King after king failed, and even though God tried to bring the nation back to the straight and narrow, they always turned back to their own evil ways. Eventually, God allowed another nation to conquer Israel and carry off most of its wealth and citizens into exile.

Daniel, one of the people taken captive, was trained to be a servant to the foreign king. But unlike so many other people, Daniel chose to follow and trust God, like Abraham. Even though he was threatened, Daniel honoured God in everything he did. He gained an incredible reputation, and men became jealous of him. They sought to kill him and had him thrown into a den of lions. The next morning, Daniel was still alive and God had proven that

He was more powerful than lions and men—and any other god. It was proven so clearly that even the heathen king began to notice.

Then there is the story of Jesus. Jesus Christ, the Son of God, was born into poverty, and grew up seeking God with all of His heart, mind, soul, and strength. He honoured God in all He did, served others, and confronted evil. Selfishness and hate had no part of Him, and others despised Him because of it. The Bible actually talks about how the people knew He was from God, but were so jealous and scared that He would take their power away from them that they decided to kill Him (John 11:46–50).

Jesus was betrayed and murdered. Evil had once again attacked the will and work of God; humanity's selfishness had robbed the world once again of what is pure and perfect. Men hated Jesus because He was loved more than they were, and because they had been exposed for the manipulators they really were. It seemed like evil had won, that the works and failures of men had simply had their way again, but God is the God of the reversal, the God of using-your-attack-against-you, the God of redemption. In their attempt to silence Jesus, they only provided another opportunity for Him to show who He was and is.

Friday He died, Sunday He was alive. He rose from the dead, and remains alive even to this day. He conquered sin and death, and used the evil intentions of humanity to bring about something so wonderful and remarkable that its waves of influence have not stopped or slowed in two thousand years.

Satan's head was crushed. The Christ had come and taken the evil intentions of man and Satan and used them to restore the image of God to mankind. This wasn't just another temporary victory over evil: this was the fulfillment of the promise. By His death and resurrection, evil was defeated—not just in action, but in the very heart and soul of mankind. The problem that continued to haunt the world was finally defeated. Men and women could now be changed! The cycle of selfishness and evil could now be stopped, because Jesus had made it possible for human nature to be remade.

God is capable of turning the evil intentions of Satan, of humanity, and of the world back on themselves to bring about good anyway. It's an incredible reversal. We see this explicitly in the New Testament when Paul says, *"...we know that in all things God works for the good of those who love him, who have been called according to his purpose"* (Romans 8:28, NIV). I don't take this statement to mean that "everything happens for a reason." No, let me be clear here: God doesn't cause sin, He doesn't cause evil, He doesn't tempt. He does, however, give people over to what they have created, and He does use our evil intentions and work around them in such a way that they backfire. Look at the story of Joseph, at the story of David, Bathsheba, and Solomon, at the story of Daniel, at the story of the crucifixion. All these stories are built around the evil intentions of men—and yet God brings about good. Even in the fall of humanity, God used the newly broken human being to be the vessel through which the Saviour came. God changes things. God restores things. God fixes and redeems and blesses and destroys deception to bring a reversal.

This is the Gospel, and it is still at work today.

Many of us have experienced days that we thought would ruin the rest of our lives—whether the day when you found out your wife had cheated on you, when you discovered that you had MS, when you got home to find out that your brother had been killed in a car crash, or when you lost your job. Perhaps you've experienced a day when you felt the sharp sting of evil caused by a lie that caught up to you, when you made a one-time mistake with a coworker, when you got scammed, or when your addiction finally took a toll on your health and marriage. But God is the God of the reversal. Some of those days have come and gone, and we see that somehow things turned around. Somehow, some of those situations were changed so much that we almost feel like we are better off now than we were before they happened. Other days haven't turned around, and evil still has a bitter sting. But God will win, and will redeem, and will bring a reversal.

"Where, oh death, is your victory? Where, oh death, is your sting?"

The sting of death is sin, and the power of sin is the law. But thanks be to God! He gives us the victory through our Lord Jesus Christ.

—1 Corinthians 15:55–57, NIV

Joni Eareckson Tada became paralyzed at a young age and now lives a vibrant life as a speaker and author, influencing the lives of those who will listen. She is still paralyzed, and remains in a great amount of pain, but looks forward to the day when she will see God complete His transformation of her in the fullness of His Kingdom. God took the frailty of her body, caused by the sin of Adam, and used it to change lives.

Chuck Colson was sent to prison for his role in the Nixon Watergate scandal. He decided to follow Christ while incarcerated, and spent the rest of his life sharing the hope of forgiveness and change with the world through speaking and writing. God took his sin and not only forgave him, but used it to open doors that allowed him to speak into thousands of lives.

Nicky Cruz, an ex-gang member, became a follower of Christ and sought to reach the people who were stuck in the same situations he had been in. His story is told in the book *The Cross and the Switchblade.*[8] God reversed the direction of his life, and used him to bring hope and life to those in the grip of poverty and violence.

John Newton actively participated in the stealing and transporting of humans for the purposes of selling them into slavery. Eventually he came to surrender his life to Christ and penned a hymn that is world-famous. He spoke of the "Amazing Grace" God had to forgive even a man like him, and use him to fight evil. He became a great supporter of William Wilberforce, the man who led the charge in the abolition of the slave trade. God brought the reversal.

Paul of Tarshish, a devout Jew bent on removing the plague of Christianity from the earth, had an encounter with Jesus on his way to imprison more Christians. Paul became one of Christianity's greatest proponents, and wrote nearly sixty percent of the New Testament. He began by persecuting Christians, and eventually was beheaded in Rome for being one. God took this man's passion for hate and turned it around to share hope.

Corrie Ten Boom sheltered Jews from the Nazis in WWII before she was caught and imprisoned. Her father and sister died in prison, and she was released due to a clerical error just before all the prisoners were killed. Years later, she met one of the men who had been a Nazi guard at that prison. Despite all she had gone through, she forgave him, and now her story has inspired people around the world. God is the God of the reversal.

Moses was just a little boy whose mother loved him so much that she risked her life to hide him from infanticide. When the king ordered all the baby boys killed, she hid Moses in a basket and set him in the river, and somehow God brought him to the king's palace where he was raised. God would eventually use him to free the Israelites from their slavery. Where one man intended to destroy a people, God reversed it and brought about the Exodus.

We see this still happen today in our own lives.

Maybe your past experience with drugs has helped you keep others from going down that path.

That messed up relationship you hated actually produced a beautiful baby girl.

Watching what divorce did to your parents led you to fight for your marriage and kept your family together.

That time of suffering you went through made you focus more on God, and helped you get through your next struggle with confidence.

That's the God of the Exodus. He is the God who takes the evil of oppression and slavery, the evil of stubborn genocidal tyrants, and uses the situation to show that He alone will fight for us. The God who says this world, with all its sin and death, isn't all we have, and we don't have to follow its pattern anymore. Not a God of evil, but a God who can actually free us from sin and death despite all of its efforts to keep us bound. He is the God who takes our mistakes and our failures, and is still able to fix them and give us life. He is the God who takes our hate and evil intentions and brings about situations that, beyond comprehension, can somehow almost be better than if we hadn't made those mistakes in the first place. God is so powerful that He takes the intentions of evil and turns the situation around to serve His purposes instead.

Would everything have been better without evil? Would things work smoother and be more peaceful, joyful, excellent, and lovely without evil? Yes. But, that's not the situation we're in right now, so we must hold tightly to the promise that even though evil will bruise us, God is able to crush its head. He is able to take our faults and failures, and bring a reversal.

While mowing the lawn a few years ago, I was listening to a podcast of Howard Hendricks speaking at a Catalyst Conference in Atlanta, and he said some things that were incredibly insightful. One thing in particular has stuck with me ever since: "[You must] develop an incurable confidence in God's ability to change people."[9]

Our God isn't powerless to defeat evil, and He isn't sitting by just letting it happen. He is living and active. He is at work, and even now is turning things around. That's the reversal. That's the Gospel. That's what the Old Testament looked towards, and that's what Jesus brought.

Evil isn't winning. Our God is—but there's a lot of work to be done. Are you ready to play your part?

CHAPTER NINE

EXPERIENCE

Sharing this good news about Jesus and the Gospel is tough. Have you ever tried to share your faith with someone just to have them ignore you or throw it back in your face? Maybe someone once tried to share their faith with you, and you thought they were nuts. Maybe you've seen one of these guys who wears a slightly offensive t-shirt about how if you don't go to church you're going to hell. One way or another, the attempts fall flat, and no one changes.

Just because we say it loudly, doesn't make us right.

John Mayer knew this and wrote a song about it called "Belief."[10] (You can listen to it online easily enough.)

We are in an era of "postmodernism." It is not completely different from modernism, but more the next step in the philosophical journey of thought that we as humans have been travelling on. It presents us with some interesting and fresh opportunities and also some frustrating and aggravating challenges. The error that pervades this philosophical trend is actually the same as the error that we found in modernism: the wrong first.

I remember the first time I realized what was going on philosophically in our world. I had studied and observed a shift from a rational and universal set of truths to a more subjective and changing idea of truth, but I didn't really understand it until one day sitting in class. I was taking an intensive course on preaching holiness. We sat in a classroom all week, and then at the end of the week had to present our sermon, and then write papers on a couple of books we had read. It was actually quite a good course.

Two of the ideas we spent time studying in the class were culture and philosophy. It was a standard discussion and expression of the shift from modernism to postmodernism—I had heard it a hundred times already, and even shared it with others, but there was something about the discussion that day which made things a little clearer.

That day, I realized how we had come to this point. Modernism was a philosophy that was based on humanity's ability to accomplish and explore. We could solve the world's problems through science, religion, politics, philosophy, and education. We humans had the ability to change the world through these things... or at least that's what we thought until we found what science, religion, politics, philosophy, and education really gave us.

Science was supposed to cure disease and give us the answers to our most valued questions, but instead we got the atom bomb, WWI and WWII, and an evolutionary perspective based on chance and not purpose.

Religion was supposed to give us freedom, meaning, innocence, and stability, but instead we got legalism, judgment, hate, shallow societies, and a group of leaders known for hypocrisy and pedophilia.

Politics was supposed to give a voice to every man, woman, and child, providing the lines through which the little guy could always be heard, and his needs met. But instead we got an upper-class society of the rich and famous riddled with scandals, under-the-table deals, and a pervasive idea that all politicians are liars and full of empty promises.

Philosophy was supposed to help us think and understand the world around us, giving insight and expression to our world, but instead we got emptiness filled with large ideas and complicated perspectives that centered on the human person who is here one day and gone the next.

Education was supposed to free our minds and unleash our potential, enabling all the peoples of the world to accomplish whatever they set their minds to, but instead we got a school system without discipline, a society of problem-enablers, a generation without a valuable work ethic, practical knowledge, or legacy, filled with children and adults who have no idea who they are, what to do, or how to actually make progress.

We were told one thing, and something else happened. We were raised to believe in what people told us and what the books said, and we discovered something different. We had a society that thought humanity's potential and word were the basis of our greatest future, and we found that instead they were the foundation of lies and death. Words are cheap. The ideas and truths of the past are cheap too.

Today, everything must be verified before it can be trusted. It must be verified through experience. Actually, experience is the *only* thing that counts. Experience is verified the moment it happens. The explanation and meaning of the experience may take investigation, the depths of it and the different aspects of the event may need more thought and further attention, but the experience happened. When something happens to you, you know it happened. I can argue until I'm blue in the face, but if you experienced it, there is really nothing I can do to disprove or discredit it. It is your belief, your experience, and when it comes down to a challenge between objective truth in ideas and your own experience, experience trumps everything.

If I experience one thing and you experience something different, you cannot argue with me and tell me that I didn't experience what I did, and I cannot argue with you and tell you that you didn't experience what you did. We may have some discussion as to what it means or what the cause was, but when it comes down to it, we have both had experiences, and nothing anyone says can take that experience away. It happened, and it was verified the moment it happened.

Some people have had the experience that Buddhism brings strength and peace, and others have experienced that Islam, Judaism, or Christianity bring meaning and purpose. That has been their experience, and no philosophical, scientific, educational, political, or religious argument can change that experience. These arguments may have truth in them—they may be completely true—but on their own they are worthless. In our postmodern world, we have had enough of empty arguments that lack verified experience. Words are cheap. We have learned not to trust them. Our own rational, emotional, relational, philosophical, physical, religious and educational experience defines us. Until we experience something different, we will not be swayed. Our experience trumps everything.

This conclusion was simply the logical outcome. When we base everything on humanistic idealism, the only constant is individual perception. At the height of modernism, we thought that we could achieve everything. If we had the technology, we could rebuild a man and then take flight on the Enterprise. We made our starting point our own selves, and created a world that is completely relative. We based everything on ourselves, and now that's the only thing we dare trust. This is simply our current situation.

This is the world we live in.

Truth is useless on its own. Experience is what carries weight in our world now.

Experience trumps everything.

Outside of experience, nothing matters.

But...

Outside the truth, nothing has value.

It says in Ephesians 4:15 (NIV) that we are to speak *"the truth in love."* In other words, we are to back up our words with action.

We need the idea with the evidence. We need the statement with the experience. Truth and experience need to go hand-in-hand.

An experience without the truth is shallow and subjective to the point of having no meaning. The truth without experience is too distant and subjective to the point of having no application. So, now we have to ask the question, why are we talking about this? How does this affect the message of Christ, and the ideas of this book? Why have I dug into it here? Because if we are to know God and share God with others, we need to understand that even though we have truth in the Bible quite readily and abundantly, experience trumps everything.

I've encountered very few people, if any, who have been convinced to follow Christ by hearing a scientific or rational argument for the Bible's truth. I'm not saying arguments aren't valuable or useful, because they very much are. For a person who is open and searching, they can be extremely enlightening and helpful, but on their own, they will fall flat.

Converts to the philosophy of Christianity remain just that: converts to philosophy. We aren't interested in converting people to philosophy or to a certain political point of view. We are interested in change, in transformation, in the truth bringing people to life from the inside out, not the outside in. Knowing a lot about a person may be great, but it isn't a relationship and it isn't really useful. Lots of people know lots about celebrities, but they don't have a relationship with them, they don't have a connection with them, and when it comes down to it, they don't know them at all. Truth without experience doesn't matter.

So how are we supposed to reach people?

Experience.

Experience has two incredible effects:

1. Those who are dead set against this Christian thing, can be radically changed despite their feelings, arguments, and previous ideas, through a legitimate experience.

2. Those who are interested in Christ will finally understand what it means to know Him as they begin an actual relationship.

They must experience God. They *must* experience God. This doesn't mean they need to see Him or hear Him, but they must experience Him somehow. They have to interact with Him in some way.

Now, we need to take a moment to look at two dynamics that must both be present if God is to have any meaning to us. We must understand God as both *big* and *close*.

What I mean by big and close are His transcendence and His immanence. God is far above us in power, size, strength, wisdom, knowledge, perfection, and so on. Yet God is also intimately and intrusively close to us in creation, in relationship, in worship, in thought, and in love. God is holy and God is knowable. God is all-knowing and God is willing to listen to us. God is all-powerful and God is relatable. He is both *big* and *close*.

If God was only transcendent and not immanent, we would be lost. He would be large, but so distant and far off that He would have no impact or influence on our lives; He wouldn't matter to us. Some people in history have argued that this is who God is: a being who is all-powerful, but has simply set the universe in motion and stepped back to watch things fly apart, never to interact or communicate with it again. If this were true, God would be like a distant star in the sky. He would be immensely powerful and strong, but because He is so far away, He would never affect us, our planet, gravity, or anything else. We wouldn't even know He was there until the night, and then He would be hard to find in the midst of all the other specks.

If God was only immanent and not transcendent, we would be lost as well. He would be intimate and relatable, but so pathetic and powerless that He would be useless. Some people have thought this way as well. They consider God to be all-loving, gentle, and kind, not harsh or judging in any way, shape, or form. To them, God takes the form of whatever belief we desire because He just wants to be with us—whether that is a relationship through Buddhism, nature, or Christianity. If this were true, God would be like a good pair of underwear, always close and comfortable but never affecting anything except your own butt. He would be like Mars—an object of intrigue to some, something they may wish to investigate out of curiosity, but they would never be affected by anything they found there. He would be quite close, but so inanimate and powerless that He would never affect us, our planet, gravity, or anything else. We probably wouldn't even notice He was there because He would be so boring.

Yet, what if God had both transcendence and immanence? What if He was both *big* and *close*?

Then we would end up with something like a star in our own solar system—our own Sun. An object of such intensity and proximity that it actually holds our planet and several others in place, circling around it over and over and over again, never to escape from its gravity. The light given off from Him would be so intense that even when reflected back to us by the moon it could light up our surroundings. He would be so intense and near that if we were to go outside on a summer's day not clothed properly, we would get burned. He would be able to warm our planet enough to give all organic life the energy necessary to exist. He would be so close and powerful that we couldn't look right at Him without causing harm to our eyes. We wouldn't be able to miss Him.

God is both big and close. Unlike a fire far away that doesn't matter, or a spark up close that has no value, God is like a bonfire at our feet, so near and intense that we may need to take a step back from the heat. He is both holy and intimate.

He must be both in our worship.

He must be both in our relationships.

He must be both in how we live our lives.

He must be both in our actions.

If He isn't, He either doesn't matter or He doesn't have any value, which means He doesn't affect us.

But He is both, and He does matter and have value, and He does affect us.

He is both personal—being—and holy—powerful.

People must experience Him as both if they are to be changed. In our world of postmodern thought, of mistrust and relativism, the only thing that will convince anyone of God and bring about a necessary shift from being self-centered to God-centered is a real experience of God.

So, am I saying this in order to let us off the hook of evangelizing and sharing our faith, because trying to argue rationally with someone to convince them is useless? No, even though rational arguments don't matter unless they are backed up with experience (we don't trust just words any more). Am I saying this in order to make you feel like everything is up to God and until He brings people to Himself despite our interactions, our work is pointless? No, though He does have to draw them.

What am I trying to say then? You were made to be the image of God.

How are people going to interact with and experience God? Through Him living in and through you. Jesus lived our life, died our death, and then was raised to life so that we could live His life starting right now. Jesus, after His resurrection, left the earth—ascended to heaven—with a promise that He would be sending the Holy Spirit to us.

...I tell you the truth: it is to your advantage that I go away, for if I do not go away, the Helper will not come to you. But if I go, I will send him to you.
—Jesus, speaking in John 16:7, ESV

But the Helper, the Holy Spirit, whom the Father will send in my name, he will teach you all things and bring to your remembrance all that I have said to you.
—Jesus, speaking in John 14:26, ESV

Truly, truly, I say to you, whoever believes in me will also do the works that I do; and greater works than these will he do, because I am going to the Father... And I will ask the Father, and He will give you another Helper, to be with you forever, even the Spirit of truth, whom the world cannot receive, because it neither sees him nor knows him. You know him, for he dwells with you and will be in you.

—Jesus, speaking in John 14:12, 16–17, ESV

For where two or three are gathered in my name, there am I among them.

—Jesus, speaking in Matthew 18:20, ESV

In the same way, let your light shine before others, so that they may see your good works and give glory to your Father who is in heaven.

—Jesus, speaking in Matthew 5:16, ESV

Keep your conduct among the Gentiles honorable, so that when they speak against you as evildoers, they may see your good deeds and glorify God on the day of visitation.

—Peter, writing in 1 Peter 2:12, ESV

In those days ten men from the nations of every tongue shall take hold of the robe of a Jew, saying, "Let us go with you, for we have heard that God is with you."

—God, speaking in Zechariah 8:23, ESV

Therefore be imitators of God, as beloved children. And walk in love, as Christ loved us and gave himself up for us, a fragrant offering and sacrifice to God.

—Paul, writing in Ephesians 5:1–2, ESV

Do not lie to one another, seeing that you have put off the old self with its practices and have put on the new self, which is being renewed in knowledge after the image of its creator.

—Paul, writing in Colossians 3:9–10, ESV

We were made to reflect the glory of God and be the image of God to the universe. Because of our sin, we lack the ability to do that, but because of the work of Christ and the gift of the Holy Spirit, we can be the image of God once again. This is what the Church is. I don't mean the building, and I don't mean a group of people who call themselves the church simply because of tradition. I mean the Church, the real group of people who actually are alive through the life of Jesus, the people who have received the Holy Spirit and are being remade into His image.

Remember my diagram of the Church: right relationship between God, me, and you. This is the Church. When people interact with this, they are interacting with the image of God. Because of the presence of God in us and in our relationships, because of the Holy Spirit in us and in our community, when people interact with us, they are interacting with God—they are experiencing God.

If we believe that Christ sent the Holy Spirit, we believe that He has given us the power and immanence to be the image. This means we are equipped to do the incredible things we were designed and built to do. It also means that we aren't alone—that many others are working beside us. It means that the Holy Spirit is here and working on us, just as He is working on the people we interact with before we meet them, when we are with them, and long after we leave.

This doesn't let us off the hook; it actually makes us more responsible. This is the point. This is the goal. Not simply to convince people about God, but to engage them as they were meant to be engaged. It is to be the image of God and love others as God loves them, watch them experience the God of the Exodus and be freed from sin just like the Israelites were freed from their slavery, and watch as they become the image of God, loving God and loving others as Jesus did. This is the point.

It has to be done intentionally and consistently. We don't accidently follow God and submit to Him, and we can't do it sporadically. If we are to show the image of God, be the image of God, glorify Him, it has to be done on purpose and it has to be done all the time, or else we are just like all the other fads with good ideas and empty results.

We have got to live out this image, and not just think about it. Because even though it may be true, and valuable, outside of experience it doesn't matter.

To change the world...

To see people saved and transformed...

To reach the lost...

The world has to experience God. And we are the Body of Christ.

CHAPTER TEN

A MATTER OF LIFE AND DEATH

If it quacks like a duck, swims like a duck, and walks like a duck, it's a duck.

Apples come from apple trees. Oranges come from orange trees. If we walk up to a tree and there are oranges on it, it must be an orange tree. If we think it is an orange tree, but there are apples growing on it, it must be an apple tree.

So then, why is it that we are supposedly the Body of Christ but so often act nothing like Him?

Pride.

If there is one thing that hinders humanity more than anything else, it is pride. Although we can all easily quote the cliché, "pride comes before a fall," and are all apt to be annoyed by someone who displays arrogance or some sort of chauvinistic tendency, nearly all of us suffer from holding a double standard. We hate the idea of pride in others, but then praise it in ourselves, or at least are blind to it in ourselves. It is a hidden and devastating cancer that so stealthily infects each part of our lives, often under the guise of healthy esteem and proper freedom. It is the single most stubborn characteristic of the human race, a characteristic that consistently keeps us focused on becoming who we want to be, rather than becoming who God designed us to be.

Okay, I'm getting uncomfortable again. I wish this no-nonsense philosophy was just a whimsical thought used to make a single point early on (can I go back to the Matrix now?). But I can't dance around what we need to talk about, and I don't think there is any value in attempting to make it more appealing or easy to swallow than it really is. We gain nothing by playing games, especially with the matter of pride. It is pride that leads us to justify evil, to ignore experience, to take for ourselves, and, incredibly, even to rebel against that which we know is true.

As C.S. Lewis has written, "the doors of hell are locked on the *inside*."[11]

It is pride that keeps us from embracing one of the most basic truths of Jesus' teaching, one often overlooked despite the popularity of John 3:16. We hardly ever consider the context when thinking about this verse, and most people don't even realize what Jesus was actually talking about when He said it. It wasn't a public speech, and it wasn't a sermon proclaimed to the disciples. It was a frank and honest conversation between two men about the ways of God and salvation. It was a conversation between Jesus and a Pharisee, a man who followed every rule he could think of. Here it is:

> *There was a man of the Pharisee sect, Nicodemus, a prominent leader among the Jews. Late one night he visited Jesus and said, "Rabbi, we all know you're a teacher straight from God. No one could do all the God-pointing, God-revealing acts you do if God weren't in on it."*
>
> *Jesus said, "You're absolutely right. Take it from me: Unless a person is born from above, it's not possible to see what I'm pointing to—to God's kingdom."*
>
> *"How can anyone," said Nicodemus, "be born who has already been born and grown up? You can't re-enter*

your mother's womb and be born again. What are you saying with this 'born-from-above' talk?"

Jesus said, "You're not listening. Let me say it again. Unless a person submits to this original creation—the 'wind-hovering-over-the-water' creation, the invisible moving the visible, a baptism into a new life—it's not possible to enter God's kingdom. When you look at a baby, it's just that: a body you can look at and touch. But the person who takes shape within is formed by something you can't see and touch—the Spirit—and becomes a living spirit.

"So don't be so surprised when I tell you that you have to be 'born from above'—out of this world, so to speak. You know well enough how the wind blows this way and that. You hear it rustling through the trees, but you have no idea where it comes from or where it's headed next. That's the way it is with everyone 'born from above' by the wind of God, the Spirit of God."

Nicodemus asked, "What do you mean by this? How does this happen?"

Jesus said, "You're a respected teacher of Israel and you don't know these basics? Listen carefully. I'm speaking sober truth to you. I speak only of what I know by experience; I give witness only to what I have seen with my own eyes. There is nothing secondhand here, no hearsay. Yet instead of facing the evidence and accepting it, you procrastinate with questions. If I tell you things that are plain as the hand before your face and you don't believe me, what use is there in telling you of things you can't see, the things of God?

"No one has ever gone up into the presence of God except the One who came down from that Presence, the Son of Man. In the same way that Moses lifted the serpent in the desert so people could have something to see and then believe, it is necessary for the Son of Man to be lifted

up—and everyone who looks up to him, trusting and expectant, will gain a real life, eternal life.

"This is how much God loved the world: He gave his Son, his one and only Son. And this is why: so that no one need be destroyed; by believing in him, anyone can have a whole and lasting life. God didn't go to all the trouble of sending his Son merely to point an accusing finger, telling the world how bad it was. He came to help, to put the world right again. Anyone who trusts in him is acquitted; anyone who refuses to trust him has long since been under the death sentence without knowing it. And why? Because of that person's failure to believe in the one-of-a-kind Son of God when introduced to him.

"This is the crisis we're in: God-light streamed into the world, but men and women everywhere ran for the darkness. They went for the darkness because they were not really interested in pleasing God. Everyone who makes a practice of doing evil, addicted to denial and illusion, hates God-light and won't come near it, fearing a painful exposure. But anyone working and living in truth and reality welcomes God-light so the work can be seen for the God-work it is."

—John 3:1–21, MSG

Jesus fleshes out this beautiful picture of how humanity, people, can have a fresh start, being remade, born anew without any of the baggage or scars of the past holding them back, and then closes with the haunting insight that many have seen this hope and still chosen to run from it. In fear of having to look at ourselves in the mirror without rose-coloured glasses, and in terror of being exposed for what we really are, we have hidden from the very light we require to see. We are like Shelob in *Lord of the Rings*, a monster hidden in the darkness waiting to consume anything that enters her reach, fed by the darkness and terrified of the light.[12] We are consumed by the fear of what may take place if ever we saw with unveiled faces, and recoil from even the suggestion that we may not be in charge.

Have you ever been told not to do something, and even had good reason to follow said instruction, but did it anyway simply out of spite? Have you ever rejected an idea, regardless of its merit, just because you didn't like who came up with it? Have you ever chosen to ignore a piece of advice because you feared what changes it might bring, and so found yourself trapped by your same old shortcomings because the cost to fix them was too high?

This is the crisis we're in. We want the benefits of the life of Jesus, but we want control of our own lives. But two lives cannot exist in a single person. One cannot have both his old life and his new life at once. We cannot be both our own and God's. In essence, we cannot be born-again without first dying. In this matter it isn't like physical death, which may be far less terrifying for many of us than what must actually happen. Here the death we face is of "my way." It is the death of the power to control our own lives and determine for ourselves who we are and what we should do. It is the death of the "me I want to be," so the "me God desires to be" can be. Even as I write this, it is apparent how intensely offensive and terrifying this is. I feel as if I should run to the shade.

But to try living two different lives is to be torn in two directions. It is one of the most awful feelings of this life. It is confusing, depressing, frustrating, and generally makes us feel lost and terrible whatever we do. It's like there is a war raging inside your stomach and heart, and Christ made it clear when He said, *"No one can serve two masters"* (Matthew 6:24, NIV).

We cannot honour God and ourselves. We can't do it. The two lives contradict each other. It would be like saying we both eat meat and won't eat meat... they are mutually exclusive; we can't do both. We can't both have our old selfish, self-run, self-ruled life, and the life of Christ in us. We have to die.

Again, I don't mean we have to die physically; I mean we have to kill the old way of living. Our old lifestyles must die. We have to give up control of our lives and surrender control to God. We must utterly remove and do away with our selfishness. We must kill our pride. We can no longer be the master of our lives, because only when that takes place can the life of Christ come in and resurrect us to the life and persons we were created to be. Only then can He resurrect our hearts, natures, personalities, gifts, abilities, talents, dreams, ideas, motives, attitudes, thoughts, goals, relationships, and purposes.

But maybe that's too high a cost.

The reality is that some aren't willing to say that there is anything wrong with their hearts, lives, goals, or actions.

They don't care to have someone else define who they are, even if that person is God.

The idea of being subjected to the will and control of God is so terrifying for some that they would gladly embrace Hell to escape it.

No one will tell them whom they can and can't sleep with.

No one will tell them what gender they are or what to do with their bodies.

No one will control where they work, or how they spend their money.

No one will determine their schedule, what they watch, what they listen to, or where they go.

No one will define them, put them in a box, or express what they are good at.

No one will limit them, and no one will take credit for what they have accomplished.

No one will keep them from loving who they want to, or hating who they need to.

I ache knowing this, and knowing how I have felt the same way at different times of my life concerning different things. But there is another way.

It is a matter of humility. Humility is what leads the way to life because it recognizes our insignificance, our frailty, our baggage, our faults and failures, our insecurities, our selfishness, and our incompleteness.

Humility is the realization of just how insignificant we are in our size, influence, and time. I'm not old, and yet I'm already confronted with the limitation of my mortality and just how short my time on earth will be. Even if I'm to live into my eighties, I will have lived in two centuries and two millennia, and yet will be forgotten by some the moment I leave their presence and by others after only a few short years. If I were to radically change the world, create a new device, or write a literary work hailed as a masterpiece around the world, it would still only take moments until someone else came along and did something recognized as more significant. I won't be able to argue for my work or continue to expand it once I am gone, and I could be killed in the blink of an eye by something as seemingly harmless as choking on a peanut, slipping on some ice, being hit by a driver who took half a second to look at their phone, or even an illness in the brain that I was never made aware of. Our frailty is startling!

Humility is the understanding that we're powerless to change anyone, including ourselves. Despite all of the self-help books, weight-loss plans, motivational speakers, and sociological and psychological studies, we always revert to the lowest level habit and action. Behaviours can be modified, relationships can be changed, ideas can be conceived, but when our guard is down, we always go back to the things we tried to run from.

When I'm tired, I start to worry and get my anxiety back. When I'm hungry, I lose my patience. When I get frustrated with people, I forget about my hope and fall back into depression.

When the environment and circumstances aren't just right, we go back to our old habits, whether they involve porn, anxiety, being rude, ignoring people, feeling we're entitled to something, eating too much, or just being lazy. Humanity by itself will always hold the same pattern. By ourselves, we will always look out for "me" first. When pushed enough, what's inside always comes out.

This understanding brings into sharp focus the fact that we've all fallen from the glory of God (Romans 3:23). We've all chosen to reject Him and His ways. We've riddled our lives with vile acts and intentions that have garnished us with incredible baggage, and have served to assault those around us. We were given a task, and have instead committed treason. We've betrayed friends, cursed our parents, violated trust, and turned the sacred romance of marriage into a vulgar pastime crafted for thoughts and actions alike. We've disobeyed laws, complained about those who act just like us, attempted to overpower and dominate in order to gain a measure of peace, and ignored what's really important. We've lied, cheated, stolen, murdered, abused, judged unfairly, beaten, raped, turned a blind eye to those in need, falsely accused, ridiculed, and hoarded. These things aren't to be taken lightly—no matter how long ago nor how trivial they may have seemed—for even the slightest act of sin in our lives has lasting consequences, regardless of how it may have been partially remedied on our part. We can't fix all that we have done.

It is when we begin to grasp all of this that a true sense of desperation crashes upon our hearts. I do not wish to dismiss this, undercut it, downplay its weight, or in any way lessen its sting. Because only when we are desperate do we actually understand how much we need someone outside of ourselves. It is only then that humility takes hold and is allowed to kill our pride and put our lives in the hands of another. It is only then that we find ourselves in a place where we are willing to say to God, "I am at your mercy."

I am at your mercy.

If you wish for me to die, I will die, for I have no other alternative nor ability.

If you wish for me to dance, I will dance.

If you wish for me to crawl, I will crawl.

If you wish for me to be free, I will be free.

If you wish for me to face this temptation, I will face it.

If you wish for me to sell everything, I will.

If you wish for me to fail at a task, I will.

If you wish for me to give up my rights, I will.

If you wish for me to be punished, so be it, for I am at your mercy.

And if you wish for me to be forgiven and reborn anew, so be it, for I am yours to do with as you please.

In the hands of anyone else, this would be utterly horrifying, and for some, even in the hands of God it brings a terror unlike anything they have ever dreamed. But it is the nature of faith, for faith is dependence. For too long we have belittled faith as a matter of mental assent or blind dogmatic ritual and philosophy, ignoring the true nature of putting our lives into the hands of one we do not see for a future we have not grasped.

It is actually the dependence on God for an unseen future that is more challenging than mentally believing in a being we have not physically seen. This is why the writer of Hebrews says, *"...faith is confidence in what we hope for and assurance about what we do not see"* (Hebrews 11:1, NIV). To be dependent upon God is similar to putting our full weight on a chair, where if it holds strong or breaks determines what happens to us. Or, perhaps it's more similar to riding in a car with someone else driving, where their actions determine where we go and in what condition we get there—we are at their mercy. In letting them drive, we relinquish our right to our own desires and will, much as would occur if we were to actually die—having no longer any power or thought in this world. It would be an almost morbid idea, were it not graced—and by that I truly mean undeserved favour—so beautifully by a God who forgives, initiates love, sacrifices, and seeks to take a diseased corpse of a being and give it remarkable, full life.

Reaching this point in our lives paves the way for a fresh start. Many of us only partially grasp this, and only begin our journey of life. We should spend the rest of our days allowing this process to work throughout every part of our hearts, minds, and souls until it takes over everything we are. Regardless, if Christ is to bring new life to us, the old life must die. We must have faith. We must be dependent. We must be at His mercy. This is an incredible contrast to our culture, but one that opens us up to real life.

Imagine the life of Adam and Eve in the garden of Eden. Imagine the innocence of a newborn child. Imagine the perfection and unique expression of untainted life. Take all the baggage we've carried and allowed to weigh us down, and move past it. Think about being forgiven for what we've done, and being graced with a forgiveness that endures even when we continue to fall short. Consider what it would be like to have old habits die and new habits overwhelm. For old grudges, motives, and attitudes to be squashed, and forgiveness, love, and hope to replace them. For peace to replace turmoil and anxiety. For understanding and endurance to grow instead of bitterness and impatience. For purity of thought and motive to overtake our actions in such a way that even when we get the action wrong, we can know it was only an error, a mistake, and not an expression of our hearts. (For example, buying a pizza for someone we didn't know was allergic to wheat. We didn't know they couldn't eat it, so even if the action was wrong, our motive was to bless.)

This is the life Jesus wants for us, because it is a life that reflects Him. Dependence is the foundation upon which we have our broken will replaced with His glorious will and our broken life replaced with His perfect life. In dependence—or faith—our money, family, career, skills, abilities, habits, perspectives, emotions, relationships, motives, actions, and purpose are transformed, changed, rebuilt, to express Jesus. We become a unique expression of who He is.

He can and will equip us to do things we could never have done on our own, and many things we never thought could ever be accomplished. And as He works in us and in others, individuals and communities of believers, the Church actually becomes the Body of Christ. We become the physical expression of Jesus on earth now. (We aren't Jesus; we simply express Him by His transforming us by the Holy Spirit through our dependence on Him. More on this in Chapter Thirteen.)

He will take over our lives, our personalities, our gifts, our habits, our relationships, and our communities to make them reflect Himself. This is why Jesus left His disciples and sent the Holy Spirit—so the Holy Spirit could take His life and fill us to the point that He overflows and spills out of us. Like a pool filled with too much water, so will our lives spill the Holy Spirit all around us. Jesus likened the Kingdom of God to a mustard seed, which starts out small and then expands to become one of the largest garden plants (Mark 4:31–32). The Holy Spirit will come in small and then grow, expanding into every dark corner of our hearts and lives, until He fills us and brings colour back to our frame.

This colour, when it comes right down to it, is what Paul refers to as the *"far better way"* (1 Corinthians 12:31, MSG). It is *agape*. 1 Corinthians 13, often referred to as the "Love Chapter," isn't simply a message for couples at their wedding. It is the culmination of our design, our purpose, and our image. It says in 1 John 4 that God is love, and so, since we have been fashioned after the image of this God, we too are designed to love—to love in thought, word, deed, and motive (1 John 4:16).

Now, many would deny that Christ can remake us entirely, simply because they don't understand it or are afraid of it. But what if that's why He came? What if the motives in all our actions could be pure? What if when our actions don't communicate what is intended, or our delivery needs work, we could still be confident that our motives were completely selfless and holy? What if our habits could be good instead of bad? What if we could really live and relate to God and others, love vertically and horizontally, communicate with God through conversation and prayer, and be free from habitual, willful sin?

Granted, as life moves and changes, we'll always have things that need work, but our hearts would be straight, and our wills aligned with God. Wouldn't that be life eternal—a life gained through knowing God and His Son Jesus Christ? (See John 17:3.) Wouldn't that be salvation from sin, and the power of death, where death would hold no power of fear nor power to end? Wouldn't that be good news?

Jesus was dead and was resurrected; that resurrection power is the power He has given us in the Holy Spirit to be remade.

This is how we change what kind of tree we are. This is how we finally act like the Body of Christ.

I believe that is the resurrection that begins now and will be completed when Christ comes back for us. I believe that is the resurrection Jesus came to provide.

I believe we can be born again and be the Body of Christ if we are willing to die.

CHAPTER ELEVEN

REMEMBER THE EXODUS

Today I was working in my office and I got busy doing something when I remembered that I needed my cell phone, so I started looking around for it. Thankfully, I quickly realized it was already in my hand! Sometimes my memory is terrible!

My wife can attest to this. I don't remember how many times (there's my bad memory again!) I have lost things and spent hours and days trying to find them.

Where are my keys?

Where did I put that really expensive pen that was given to me when I graduated Bible school?

Where are those insurance papers?

What did I do with my gloves?

I feel like this is a fairly common problem, though. We are broken beings, and as broken beings, we have a tendency to forget things. Actually, I think it is probably more than a tendency, it's a habit. The things we need to remember, we forget. It's like the most important things are the ones most easily forgotten, lost, misplaced, and generally ignored. It happens naturally. They just fall out of minds and are gone. Unless I write things down and then post them in places where I will see them (but not see them so much that I begin to ignore them), I will usually forget them. There are times when I feel that if my head wasn't attached, I'd lose it.

Calendar programs, agendas, post-it notes, putting string on our fingers, voice mail messages, alarms, reminder emails, and many other resources are gifts from heaven! They help us remember the important things we can't seem to actually remember on our own. The consequences of forgetting these things are sometimes minor inconveniences, and sometimes they are frustratingly huge. This is how it has always been. When we forget the most important things, we end up in trouble. When we forget that which is most essential, we get lost, scared, confused, and quite often we either hurt someone else or hurt ourselves. It's been this way since the dawn of humanity. We are human and we forget, and usually we forget the most important things, like who we are.

In the Garden of Eden, we find that when Adam and Eve forget what is most important, they end up losing what is most important. By way of a few simple questions at the foot of the tree, doubt arose in their minds and the truth began to slip from their thoughts. Who they were, and who God was, started to fade from a vibrant image to a vague figure far in the distance. They quickly began to forget what was most important, and this was their downfall.

In contrast, we see something different happen with Jesus. When He gets to be about thirty years old, He goes out into the wilderness and is tempted directly by the deceiver, Satan, just like Adam and Eve were. In the wilderness, Satan asks Jesus a few simple questions, questions formulated to inspire doubt, questions created to help Jesus forget the most important things. Questions to make Jesus think: Is *God* really powerful enough to do what He says? Am *I* really powerful enough to do what He says? Am I really who I *think* I am? And at each question, instead of taking the question beyond what was said and allowing the truth to slip away, Jesus does something very, very important...

He remembers. He recalls Scripture and holds it tightly in His mind. He intentionally, and consistently, remembers. He remembers who He is, and He remembers who God is, and in doing this makes it through the temptation in one piece, still whole.

If Jesus had forgotten and allowed the deceiver's questions to make Him doubt who He was and who God was, things would have been much different. I believe that is what Satan was attempting to do—make Jesus doubt who He was. There was no crowd watching, nothing to prove to anyone, except maybe to Himself. These weren't simply temptations of physical relief, but temptations to prove who He was to Himself. This is what happened in the garden, this is what happens with us, but Jesus didn't need to prove anything, because He remembered.

Throughout the Old Testament, we see some people forgetting and some people remembering. In some instances, in fact most, we see people acting like Adam and Eve, forgetting what is most important. Then, in other instances, we see people acting like Jesus, remembering what is most important. This is most apparent in the history of Israel in the years following the Exodus. The people wasted no time in forgetting who God was, what He had done, and who they were to Him. After all God had done in proving that He was greater than all other powers, the people of Israel stood at the edge of the Red Sea and forgot it all. A new obstacle arose and they forgot the most important information they so desperately needed to remember.

It is remarkable how humanity can forget. After seeing God turn a river into blood, black out the sun only where He wanted to, and kill the firstborn only of those who hadn't submitted to Him, it should have been easy for the people of Israel to believe that God could take care of some water, or an army of men. But this was new territory, a new challenge, a new problem, and they doubted God, they doubted who they were to Him, and they forgot the Exodus even as they were in it.

They did the same thing when they got past the Red Sea. They got to the mountain where God was meeting with Moses, and they built idols (Exodus 32). They got to a spot where there was no water and they complained and expected to die (Exodus 17). They got to the Promised Land and they saw giants, and after all the time in the wilderness where God made it rain food, and all the works of the Exodus, they forgot and cowered in fear (Numbers 14). It took them another forty years in the wilderness to learn how to remember, and even once they had made their home in the Promised Land, we see the trend return: they forgot again.

God understood the necessity of remembering what was most important, which is why He gave His people a reminder. The Passover, the festival that took place on the night before the Israelites left Egypt, was to be repeated every year. When God gave His people the law, He also intended them to write it everywhere so they would be constantly reminded:

Hear, O Israel: The Lord our God, the Lord is one. You shall love the Lord your God with all your heart and with all your soul and with all your might. And these words that I command you today shall be on your heart. You shall teach them diligently to your children, and shall talk of them when you sit in your house, and when you walk by the way, and when you lie down, and when you rise. You shall bind them as a sign on your hand, and they shall be as frontlets between your eyes. You shall write them on the doorposts of your house and on your gates.

And when the Lord your God brings you into the land that he swore to your fathers, to Abraham, to Isaac, and to Jacob, to give you—with great and good cities that you did not build, and houses full of all good things that you did not fill, and cisterns that you did not dig, and vineyards and olive trees that you did not plant—and when you eat and are full, then take care lest you forget the Lord, who brought you out of the land of Egypt, out of the house of slavery. ...

When your son asks you in time to come, "What is the meaning of the testimonies and the statutes and the rules that the Lord our God has commanded you?" then you shall say to your son, "We were Pharaoh's slaves in Egypt. And the Lord brought us out of Egypt with a mighty hand."
—Deuteronomy 6:4–12, 20–21, ESV (I recommend reading all of chapters 6–11 to really get the point.)

They needed to remember. They needed to celebrate the Passover every year so they would remember. They needed the Passover so they would always, always, remember the Exodus. It is in the Exodus that God showed the world who He is, and who we are. Remember Exodus 14:14? *"The Lord himself will fight for you. Just stay calm"* (NLT).

If you examine Israel's history, you will find that when they didn't celebrate the Passover, they ended up in trouble and ended up going away from God. Yet, when they did celebrate the Passover, they were on track with God and they brought honour to Him. Whenever they remembered the Exodus and who God was, they were who they were supposed to be, but whenever they forgot the Exodus, they found death.

Take a look at just a few of the passages throughout the Old Testament that focus on the Exodus:

Remember that you were slaves in Egypt and that the Lord your God brought you out of there with a mighty hand and an outstretched arm. Therefore the Lord your God has commanded you to observe the Sabbath day.
—Deuteronomy 5:15, NIV

And who is like your people Israel—the one nation on earth that God went out to redeem as a people for himself, and to make a name for himself, and to perform great and

*awesome wonders by driving out nations and their gods
from before your people, whom you redeemed from Egypt?*
—2 Samuel 7:23, NIV

There are many more examples. See any of the following:
Deuteronomy 15:15, 24:18;
Joshua 9:9, 24:17;
Judges 2:12, 6:8;
1 Samuel 2:27, 10:18;
1 Kings 8:53;
Psalm 81:10;
Psalm 106:21;
Jeremiah 11:4;
Daniel 9:15;
Hosea 13:4.

Despite all of these references to the Exodus, the Israelites actually practiced the Passover as a people only a few times—namely, the following: Joshua 5:10 (at the start of their history in the Promised Land); 2 Kings 23:21 & 2 Chronicles 30:1 (a few hundred years after being in the Land); Ezra 6:19 (after they had been exiled from the land for seventy years and were finally allowed back).

Is it any wonder that the majority of kings in Israel and Judah were evil?

Remembering the Exodus is absolutely essential to staying on track and finding life. There are two practical things to do because of this. The first is to actually remember the history of the Israelites and how God proved Himself in freeing them from Egypt. The second is to remember how God has proved Himself in your own life, often referred to as your testimony. This could be when you first experienced God's forgiveness and love, or when He entered your life and began to transform you. It could be when you made a significant step in your transformation, conquering an addiction or finally being obedient with something difficult.

It could also be a time when you felt stuck, like there was no way out, or no good options, and miraculously God provided for you.

I remember when I was flying to Kentucky on my own for the first time. I was so nervous about travelling that I wanted to just run away from the airport. This story may seem really silly to many of you who are experienced travelers, but to me it was really stressful and scary. En route, the flights got changed, missed, or cancelled, but I made it to my destination. When I arrived, I felt so stupid for doubting God. I had been so worked up about travelling, and despite all of the problems that took place on the journey, He got me to my destination safely. I felt impressed with God, and humbled by my ignorance and lack of trust.

Then, on my way home, I felt confident and all the flights went well—until the last one. After a couple of hours sitting on the plane, they cancelled the flight, and it looked like I would be stranded, possibly for a couple of days. In that moment, standing in line to speak with someone who could rebook flights, I forgot everything I needed to remember. I forgot who God was. I forgot how He had provided on the way down. I forgot that He would fight for me and that I had to stay calm. And just when I was about to lose my composure, He provided yet again. Not only did He get me home, but He provided companions for the journey. Why did I forget? How could I forget? I should have remembered! We often become overcome by stress like this, but we don't have to.

And they have conquered [Satan] by the blood of the Lamb and by the word of their testimony, for they loved not their lives even unto death.
—Revelation 12:11, ESV

Blessed be the God and Father of our Lord Jesus Christ, the Father of mercies and God of all comfort, who comforts us in all affliction, so that we may be able to comfort

those who are in any affliction, with the comfort with
which we ourselves are comforted by God.

—2 Corinthians 1:3–4, ESV

It is by remembering the Exodus, and remembering our personal exodus, that we begin to remember who God is, and consequently remember who we are. The Gospel takes hold again and begins to rule in our hearts and minds and lives. When we remember, things get back on track, things get straightened out. As Paul points out in 2 Corinthians 5, knowing Christ—remembering Christ in us—clarifies our own identity.

For Christ's love compels us, because we are convinced
that one died for all, and therefore all died. And he died
for all, that those who live should no longer live for them-
selves but for him who died for them and was raised again.
So from now on we regard no one from a worldly
point of view. Though we once regarded Christ in this
way, we do so no longer. Therefore, if anyone is in Christ,
the new creation has come: The old has gone, the new is
here! All this is from God, who reconciled us to himself
through Christ and gave us the ministry of reconciliation:
that God was reconciling the world to himself in Christ,
not counting people's sins against them. And he has com-
mitted to us the message of reconciliation. We are there-
fore Christ's ambassadors, as though God were making
his appeal through us. We implore you on Christ's behalf:
Be reconciled to God. God made him who had no sin to be
sin for us, so that in him we might become the righteous-
ness of God.

—2 Corinthians 5:14–21, NIV

We see this power in remembering God's acts in our own stories.

Sometimes our stories help others deal with their own struggles, or keep them from making the same mistakes we made.

I have worked with several people, helping them teach and disciple teens who are in some pretty rough situations. These people have come from some pretty rough situations too. Some of them have dealt with drugs, addictions to porn and sex, depression, or the pain of abuse. These leaders have gone through some remarkable changes in their own lives, and continue to deal with their pasts and their ongoing struggles, but they have found that because of their experiences they have been able to speak into the lives of these teens with an empathy and clarity they otherwise would not have been able to. Their struggles have helped these teens see the truth, find freedom and practical solutions to their problems.

I knew a man who dealt with significant sexual temptation for most of his life. Christ brought healing to his past and allowed him to have power over his temptations, though they still remained. This opened many doors for him to be able to share and help others who struggled with this same dilemma—the temptation to reduce relationships and sex to a merely physical desire. He had unique insights into the struggle and was able to take a stand against the belief that if we are born a certain way, we have to live that way, which is a contradiction of the hope we all have in Christ to be free from the natural sin in our hearts.

I know another man who has faced the pain and rejection not only of divorce, but being removed from a job and a ministry position because his wife cheated on him. He is able to see how he contributed to the breakdown of the relationship, while still seeing clearly that it was his ex-wife who cheated. This has given him the ability to speak into many lives and marriages from a perspective that most pastors never have. Much of his insight and story have been helpful even in my own life.

Remembering our stories can also help us deal with the things we are facing in our own lives.

There are a couple of people I know personally who have incredibly humble spirits and a passionate willingness to grow. They are like this because they are constantly reminded of how they used to be and how much God has saved them from. They remember their pasts and so have an incredible appreciation for God's forgiveness, power to change, and ability to use them. It has set the stage for God to use them in powerful ways, and keep them seeking Him no matter what.

Our testimony becomes an incredible tool used to recall how we have faced temptation in the past and made it through. It is the reminder that we don't need the thing that is tempting us— we don't have to give in, we can say no, we can avoid it and be content. I know one girl who has struggled with a particular addiction in her life for many years, and when she is able to fight the temptation, she gets excited. When she is able to remember how she has stood against it in the past, she is able to stand against it again, and then all the shame and fear she had melts away, creating a joy so rich and full that she has to share it. When she remembers, the temptations backfire and she becomes more passionate for Christ.

I have found this in my own life, and I know a few other people who say the same thing, that when we are at school or work with a lot of big assignments on our desks the stress can be overwhelming. There have been times when I have had too many things due for the amount of time allotted, but God has provided a way for everything to get done, or for the deadlines to be extended. There have also been times when I have failed and God was still able to bring about a good result. When I remember this, the stress eases, and hope fills my heart and mind instead of fear.

Our stories need to be remembered, but we also see the power and necessity of remembering the Exodus expressed in the Bible. It is the central and fundamental event that shows us God is God and we are not, and He alone is fighting for us. It is the truth that through a sacrifice God set us free from slavery and gave us life. It is the reality that through His work—and only His work—He brought us from where we were to be with Him and make us holy. It isn't simply about the past, but about who He has made us to be. It's the message that we don't have to be slaves to anything anymore. We don't have to be bound by bad habits, self-ish motives, evil intentions, sinful actions, or even forgetfulness. All of those things can be dealt with; all of those things can be conquered. None of those things have to haunt us. They may still try to attack, and they will creep up in new and inventive ways, as life and people are constantly changing, but there is always the power to conquer them through Christ, the one the Passover lamb represented and symbolized. The Exodus was the statement that Jesus was coming to change everything.

God has shown that He is more powerful than all, and in the past He instituted a tradition that was designed to remind all the people that God would provide a way of freedom. It is a re-markable parallel to note that Jesus was crucified at a Passover celebration (Luke 22–23). Jesus is called the *"Lamb of God"* (John 1:29, NIV). He is referred to as the Passover Lamb (1 Corinthians 5:7). The actual lamb that was killed at Passover wasn't anything special. That little lamb had no power in itself, and the act had no power in itself, but it was an act of obedience and faith for the Jews to sacrifice this lamb. If they sacrificed the lamb, it showed that they trusted what God said, wanted to obey Him, and believed He would set them free. It was an act of faith looking forward to their Exodus. It was an act of faith looking forward to how God would become a man, die, and rise again, through a huge sacrifice, to set them free (Hebrews 2:14–18). And the people needed to remem-ber that. They needed to remember God was the one who would save them and set them free.

In remembering that, they were remembering the most im-portant things—things that would define everything else they did, how they thought, what plans they made, and who they were. In remembering who God was—His character, His sacrifice, His love—they would remember that they were created not to be Him, but to be like Him.

But when we forget the Exodus, we forget that we have already been forgiven and that Jesus came not just to forgive us, but to save us. We forget that God is more concerned about where we are going than what we have done, regardless of how far along in the journey we are, or how badly we mess up. We forget that God determines right and wrong and what direction we should be going. We forget that we can't control God or manipulate Him. We forget that His love is unconditional. We forget that relationship isn't unconditional. We forget that He is concerned with the vertical and the horizontal. We forget that we are defined by Him, not Him by us. We forget that God is first.

We forget who we are. We forget what it means to be human. We forget what we are supposed to be doing, and so end up running back to the slavery we so desperately needed saving from. We forget that He can defeat the sin in our lives. We forget that He can turn evil things around and somehow bring about good. We forget that there is always hope. We forget that "good" ideas aren't always what He wants. We forget that He Himself is fighting for us, and that we need to be quiet and get on board. This is why He must change our hearts, and why we must always remember the most important things:

God is first.

We are made in His image.

Remember the Exodus.

CHAPTER TWELVE

EXPLODING KINGDOM

W e've spent a good portion of this book discussing God and us. We've examined what it means to be made in the image of God—how we as persons were made to reflect Him—and studied who God is. We've seen that everything must start in the right place: with God. We've seen why that matters to us, and how that changes who we are.

But now we need to take a look at what all that means, beyond the concept of "me." Some have argued that the church has been so focused on discipleship that it forgets about evangelism. Others have argued the contrary, saying that too much focus on evangelism leads to no discipleship. In reality, we've done both, and neither. The truth is, real evangelism is part of discipleship, and is part of the sanctification process. Real evangelism leads to further discipleship. Evangelism that is free of discipleship isn't real evangelism—it's consumerism and nothing more. In this form, people come to Christ for what they can get, not to surrender to His will, design, and image. It's a form of the flimsy gospel and doesn't change people, but just leaves them dead. This isn't evangelism, it isn't good news—it's just useless.

At the same time, real discipleship is so much a part of evangelism that we cannot have the one without the other. Discipleship that is free of evangelism is empty study. Discipleship that doesn't lead to sharing the good news, loving and reaching others, giving of ourselves, surrendering our lives, and general evangelizing, isn't discipleship. If our discipleship doesn't make us more like Christ—more sacrificial, more loving, more selfless, more concerned about others, more evangelistic—whatever it is that we're doing, it isn't discipleship. Discipleship that doesn't bring us more into line with the image of God isn't discipleship. And so, to have either discipleship or evangelism without the other is to have neither.

I say all this because I don't want you to think that this book is all about us, or us and our relationship with God. I also don't want you to think that the greater part of this book discusses discipleship and now we are transitioning into a separate discussion about evangelism. No—they are inherently connected and intertwined. What we have discussed about being the image is part of being evangelistic. And what we are about to discuss about evangelism is part of discipleship. Like I said, I actually have a hard time distinguishing one from the other, for discipleship is part of evangelism, and vice versa.

To make my next point, let's talk about stars.

Stars are incredible things. The star we see most often is the one our solar system revolves around: the Sun. The Sun is like every other star in how it functions. It is an enormous mass of hydrogen that is constantly going through a process of nuclear fusion, where two hydrogen atoms combine together, releasing a staggering amount of energy as they form a new atom called helium. Here on earth we use the process of nuclear fission, where atoms are split, in our nuclear reactors, creating heat that is used to create electricity. It is also the process of nuclear fission that forms the power behind the nuclear bomb. Nuclear fusion releases even more energy than nuclear fission.

The Sun is then, essentially, constantly exploding. It's a giant ball of exploding gas. Because it's constantly exploding, it gives off intense energy that sustains life on our planet and gives light during the day and the night. Like I mentioned in a previous chapter, we are just the right distance away from the sun that we can understand the intensity of it. It produces light for us in the daytime, and that light is reflected back to us by the moon at night. We get vitamin D from sunlight, and plants capture the energy of light through photosynthesis, which in turn allows them to grow. Animals then eat these plants, and other animals eat those animals. Without the sun there would be no plants, and thus no animals. The Sun is absolutely essential to life.

But not all stars are currently functioning like our Sun. Some stars have burned out, having used up all of their fuel. The mass of the helium they've produced has been compacted into such a small space at such an enormous density that it has created what is called a black hole. The gravity of this mass is so intense that everything in its proximity is drawn into it and cannot escape. Not even light can escape the gravity of a black hole. When scientists find a black hole, they actually just find nothing. It looks like a spot in the sky where there isn't anything. But there is something there—it has just turned inward. It has imploded to such an extent that nothing and no one outside of it ever sees anything from it or gains anything from it. It is a dead star that has ceased to explode, and instead has imploded to the point that it destroys life rather than creating it.

The science of stars is the same as the reality of humanity, the Body of Christ, the Church. We are meant to explode, and when we cease to explode, we implode and destroy life. When we cease to live out *agape* and become content with meeting our own needs, our own desires, our own way of life, we turn inward, implode, and suck the light out of the world around us. Like a black hole, the Church can do more harm than good. This is why we must intentionally and consistently explode, rather than implode.

This isn't a new idea, nor is it a new warning that I am presenting. The Israelites did much the same thing that we've done in thinking that they were the objects of the blessing rather than the conduit of the blessing to others. The Lord, through the prophet Ezekiel, had this to say to them (we've seen this passage before, but it bears repeating):

> God's Message came to me: "Son of man, prophesy against the shepherd-leaders of Israel. Yes, prophesy! Tell those shepherds, 'God, the Master, says: Doom to you shepherds of Israel, feeding your own mouths! Aren't shepherds supposed to feed sheep? You drink the milk, you make clothes from the wool, you roast the lambs, but you don't feed the sheep. You don't build up the weak ones, don't heal the sick, don't doctor the injured, don't go after the strays, don't look for the lost. You bully and badger them. And now they're scattered and easy pickings for the wolves and coyotes. Scattered—my sheep!—exposed and vulnerable across mountains and hills. My sheep scattered all over the world, and no one out looking for them!
> —Ezekiel 34:1–6, MSG (emphasis in original)

This reaping from others is the culture and society that we live in today. It's the nature of our governments, our institutions, capitalism in general, and our educational system. Even a big part of how we interpret the Bible is based on this assumption. Take a look at the stories that Jesus told about the value of the Kingdom of God. There is the story of the man who found a field that had a treasure buried in it, so he sold all he had to buy the field and gain the treasure (Matthew 13:44). There is the story of the man who found the pearl of great worth and sold all he had to buy it (Matthew 13:45–46). When we read these stories, we interpret them as the Kingdom of Heaven being valuable to us, so we should get rid of everything else in order to buy into heaven. We read them and assume that it is a petition for us to see the personal value of the Kingdom.

I offer this variation of interpretation though, one that goes against our customs and culture of consumerism. Along with these two stories about the kingdom of God, Jesus also describes the Kingdom of Heaven as a mustard seed that starts out small and grows until it blesses the birds, and he says that it is like yeast that starts out in a small amount and then works its way through dough, changing how it acts and exists (Matthew 13:31–33). What if the stories of the Kingdom of Heaven are less about gaining some kind of material or eternal reward, and more about changing our views about what is most valuable? What if these stories are actually about a man who sees that the Way of Jesus, the way of serving others, is so much more valuable than materials or rewards that he completely changes his life in order to live like Christ?

There is a passage in the book of Romans that has haunted me for years. I always liked reading Romans 8; I found it inspirational, insightful, and encouraging, but I would rarely read the passages around that chapter. Yet it was the passage directly following chapter 8 that has proved to be most impacting and convicting to me in recent years. It may be the most convicting passage I have ever read. This is what it says:

> *For I could wish that I myself were accursed and cut off from Christ for the sake of my brothers, my kinsmen according to the flesh.*
> —Paul, writing in Romans 9:3, ESV

> *It's the Israelites... If there were any way I could be cursed by the Messiah so they could be blessed by him, I'd do it in a minute.*
> —Paul, writing in Romans 9:3, MSG

The author of the letter to the Romans, Paul, looks at his fellow Jews and sees how they are not following Christ, and states that if he could give up heaven—give up the change he's had in his life, be cursed and cast away from God for eternity so that the grace he's received could be passed on to those who are lost—he would do it. He would give up salvation and eternity so that someone else could have it.

Please don't just breeze over this. This isn't simply a poetic notion, and it isn't the desire of a whimsical thinker. This is a man who was a theologian of the highest degree, a man who understood the depths of separation from God that come from being accursed by Him, and he would still take it in order to bless another—another who didn't deserve it, and maybe didn't even want it. He would give up what was most precious and dear to him in all existence if it would draw others to Christ.

How many of us would do that? Let's put this beyond the present life that Christ wants to give us and consider what this would look like in the scheme of eternity: separation in Hell from God and all He is; no love, peace, joy, hope, purpose, gentleness, meaning, value, grace, security, confidence, light, freedom, or life now, tomorrow, next week, next year, next decade, on and on and on...

I hate the feeling of being without any of those attributes of God even for a day; a week of it brings deep depression; years of it can undo our minds; a lifetime can leave you lifeless and cold like a zombie driven by animal instinct. And still, Paul would willingly take that if it would mean that someone else didn't have to—so someone else could have Christ.

I don't think it's possible to give up our salvation so another can have it, but Paul's heart is such that he would if he could. Would we?

The really convicting thing about this is that I don't think this is just a novel idea that some of the great saints have. I think this is actually supposed to be the heart of every Christian, every human. If this was the heart of every person, no one would be hungry, alone, abandoned, rejected, abused, or in need. If this was the heart of the Church, we wouldn't need advertising campaigns, fundraisers, pop culture, or evangelistic programs to reach people. If this was the heart of the Body of Christ...

But it was the heart of Christ. He became human so we could be freed. His heart was to bless us rather than just fight for Himself. It was to expose His heart to such an extent that all the love inside could get out, knowing full well that He was leaving His most vital and personal aspects vulnerable to attack.

Now let's go back to the story of the man who finds treasure in a field. What if the story is talking about a man like Paul who sees this world and eternity, then finds someone who is lost and hurting and sells all he has in order to bless them, for they are more valuable than his own reward?

What if the Kingdom of God wasn't about what we could get—imploding—but was about giving—exploding. What kind of light would the Church be producing if we had the heart of Christ, the sanctified heart of Paul, exploding in us?

That's a terrifying thought. Exploding is dangerous. It's scary. It's unpredictable. It's intense. It's beyond our control. It's risky. It's an event that we cannot properly see the outcomes for.

Implosion, selfishness, consumerism: those things are safe. We can put up all the walls we want, burn whatever bridges we need to, take whatever our hearts desire and make sure we are taken care of. No one else matters when we're a black hole, as long as our own needs are met. In life, we consume other people, use relationships, scheme in business deals, manipulate emotions, and use connections all so that we can have the safety of knowing that we are taken care of.

We do these same things in the church. We become more concerned with paying the bills, having ministries that our people enjoy, using language that only those in the church can understand, sticking with music, practices, traditions, ministries, and ideas that the people who are already here like. Even when we do outreach, it's in an attempt to get people in so that we can keep the doors of the church open and continue to do things the way we like them to be done, in some kind of religious attempt to make sure there's enough money for us to coast on. It's safe. We own the rules. We build and guard the gates. No one can hurt us... at least not from the outside, but we are already a dead star inside.

The exploding kingdom is one that forces us to get rid of our walls. In order to love like Paul, like Christ, we have to allow ourselves to be completely vulnerable. The more walls we have and the more barriers there are between us and others, the less love is able to reach them. The more garbage we are carrying around with us and the more filth that is in our hearts, the harder it is to love others the way they need to be loved. It becomes increasingly necessary that we become more and more like Christ—the image of God, the Body of Christ—in order to bless others.

In the exploding kingdom, we run hard after sanctification to be the image of God—not for our own gain, but so that we can better bless others. This is dangerous, because it means there are no limits on what God can grab ahold of to get rid of or change. It means that there is no barrier around our hearts if others wish to abuse them. It means that we must rely on Christ to fight for us and provide for us in all things, and that we need to be completely confident in who Christ has made us to be, not in what others say or in what we have created on our own. It means we're exposed for all the world to see, using our hearts, our money, our families, our relationships, our work, our everything for the Kingdom. Because in the explosion, life and light can be given in such potent ways that the lost can be found.

This is how the Trinity functions. This is *agape*. This is why Christ came, to restore the image of God, and bring heaven to earth:

...your kingdom come, your will be done, on earth as it is in heaven.
—Jesus, speaking in Matthew 6:10, NIV

Then I saw "a new heaven and a new earth," for the first heaven and the first earth had passed away, and there was no longer any sea. I saw the Holy City, the new Jerusalem,

coming down out of heaven from God, prepared as a bride beautifully dressed for her husband. And I heard a loud voice from the throne saying, "Look! God's dwelling place is now among the people, and he will dwell with them. They will be his people, and God himself will be with them and be their God. 'He will wipe every tear from their eyes. There will be no more death' or mourning or crying or pain, for the old order of things has passed away."
—Revelation 21:1–4, NIV

And by the working of the Holy Spirit, the Kingdom—like a mustard seed or yeast—starts out small and then takes over our hearts and spreads to the people around us. Then the Holy Spirit works in them and spreads the Kingdom in them, and then to others around them. People are exposed to the experience of the truth of Christ, and things change—but only if we are a living star. Otherwise we run the risk of becoming like the people who Ezekiel spoke against. And, honestly, one of the greatest fears I have is that I will one day meet my Creator face to face and He will say to me what Ezekiel said, "I gave you a responsibility and instead of protecting and caring for your brothers and sisters, you used them to gain for yourself, and now they are wandering about lost. My sheep are lost, and you did nothing about it!"

Back when I began writing this book, I was alone in my apartment watching the movie *Schindler's List*. I had seen the film back in high school and gained an appreciation for it, but this time it wasn't for history class. This time I watched the movie and began to feel the emotions connected with the injustice, horror, conviction, and guilt that were wrapped up in Oskar Schindler's work to save Jews during the Holocaust of WWII. I was amazed at the sacrifices that Schindler made, and the desperation of the Jews as they faced an enemy so incredibly intent on abusing and eliminating them with passionate hatred. Then I got to one of the final scenes.

This scene left me a wreck. In the movie, something broke in Schindler, and something broke in me. He was overwhelmed by the reality that he still had resources left that could have been used to save more lives, and didn't, and I became overwhelmed by the reality that I'm doing the same thing.[13] It's a movie with lots of explicit and disturbing content, but if you can handle it, you should just go watch it. Yes, you should just go watch it—and don't even try to brace yourself for that scene where the war has ended and Schindler is about to leave. I can't effectively describe the overwhelming pain and sadness I felt in realizing that I was— we were, we are—holding onto things that could be given up to save someone's life and aren't. The value of my comfort, my money, my luxury, my plans, my pride, my secret sins, my toys was outweighing the value of someone else's eternal life.

I don't think I even managed to finish the last few minutes of the movie. I was crying uncontrollably. I wasn't crying like a baby; it was worse. I was crying some deep agonizing conviction, and it kept coming and coming and coming. I had my eyes opened and I couldn't shake it.

Oskar Schindler saved hundreds of people during the Holocaust at great personal risk to himself, and in the end (at least at the end of the film), he still saw more that he could have done. I think this man was a hero. But I fear that when we meet God at the end of our physical lives, God will graciously welcome us home, and we will be confronted on our own by the realization of what else we could have done to save one more...

We need not be driven mad by our past—God is more than capable of redeeming that—but we must consider our present and future. Will we implode and become a black hole? Will we serve others because of what we will gain from it? Or will we explode, be a shining light, and give life? Will we serve others with a heart that is willing to give up eternity with Christ so that another might take our place? Will we come to the end of our lives and think, "If I had stopped drinking, I could have reached one more person... if I had let that grudge go, I could have saved one more...

if I had gotten rid of my TV, I could have fed another person... if I had given up my taste in music, we could have reached someone else... what is the value of those things compared to another life?"

To be a Christian—to be like Christ, to be the image of God, to open ourselves up to be vulnerable so our hearts can be fully shared—is to be part of the exploding kingdom.

CHAPTER THIRTEEN

ALPHA OMEGA

So now the question is, how does all this fit together?

My brother went to Las Vegas a couple years ago, and he bought me a few souvenirs. One of them was a set of drumsticks from the Blue Man Group, another was a set of drumsticks from the Hard Rock Café Las Vegas (I can't actually play drums, I just would like to), and he also brought me home a bookmark. This bookmark was very special and unique. It was laminated, had some graphics from *The Dark Knight* on it, and contained a single frame from the movie's film strip.

It was obvious where this frame came from and what it represented. A single glance at it and I could tell what movie it was from, even without the graphics around it. I looked at it and saw the face of a villain covered in white makeup, topped with green hair, and glaring with a stretched grin. I recognized it as a picture of the Joker, and it was clearly from the movie *The Dark Knight*. It wasn't the entire film, it didn't have every scene, every aspect, or every character of the film, but it still represented the entire film. This single snapshot from the movie was a finite, limited, and yet still pure and complete, image of the film.

The film had thousands and thousands of individual frames woven together. One frame by itself wasn't the entire movie, nor did it have all of its characteristics. A full film has motion and sound, but all this image had was a single visual moment from the film. All the shapes, colours, lighting and shadow were the film's. Each frame, regardless of where it is in the entirety of the film, represents the film. And it isn't just one aspect of that snapshot that has its origin from the movie: the whole image, the entire frame, has its form and being from the movie.

When we consider who we are and who God is, we are like the single frame and God is like the entire movie. He is made up of billions and billions of individual frames, an infinite number of individual snapshots. Each snapshot is equal, not more nor less an image of God than any other snapshot. Each frame comes fully from God. It isn't just one aspect of the picture that comes from Him, but everything about it comes from Him. We are the snapshots; we are the individual frames. You are a unique, finite snapshot of God's image!

This isn't to say that we are God. We aren't God, and God is not made of us. We aren't part of His ontological being; we aren't made of the same substance He is, nor could we become the fullness of God by somehow combining ourselves. No, we are completely separate and other than God, but we are snapshots of who He is. We are images of the One God, not parts of Him.

As the image of God, it isn't just a single aspect of who you are that is supposed to reflect God. Everything about you is supposed to display His character and love. Whether you're an introvert or an extrovert, that aspect of your personality was intended to display a characteristic of God. If you're artistic, athletic, logical, authoritative, carefree, or intelligent, that aspect of your personality was intended to display a characteristic of God.

How is this possible? How can the extroverted aspect of one person and the introverted aspect of another reflect the same God? Well, first, we are all combinations of both extrovert and introvert; no one is completely one or the other, and this goes for many of our personality traits. Secondly, God is big and has a full and perfect character that can be seen in many different situations. He is both kind and just. He is both energetic and quiet. We reflect those different aspects of Him, as finite, limited snapshots of Him. He is the infinite God creating an infinite amount of finite images, each one showing who He is in many different ways, and yet also in many similar ways.

This means that everything about you was meant to glorify God. It wasn't just your moral or spiritual nature that was designed to honour God and reflect Him—everything about you was designed to do that. Yet, every aspect of who we are has been broken and tainted, so our creativity, our logic, our energy, and our thoughts aren't what they should be. It's like we are frames from a film, but all the colour has gone out of the picture and the lines have started to fade. If you look carefully you might be able to tell which movie we come from, or you might just think that where we come from is dark, cold, grey, and full of emptiness.

This is why Jesus came.

Every piece of who we are that was originally designed to reflect the perfect character of God can again reflect it. The colour can be put back. By the work of Jesus and the filling of the Holy Spirit who applies Jesus' work and life to us, we are made new. It will take time for it to touch every part of us, and the transformation won't be complete until we are free from this broken world and our broken bodies, but we can begin the transformation now and be restored now.

We can be holy. We can be sanctified. We can each be bright, pure, unique images of God. Jesus can restore us so completely that humility becomes our first reaction rather than pride and arrogance. He can change us so much that it becomes more natural for us to be selfless and righteous than to be selfish and sinful. We can become what we were created to be. We can be like Jesus— the physical presence of the image of God on earth, guiding and caring for His creation. We can be the Body of Christ. This is what Paul was talking about in 1 Corinthians 12:

What I want to talk about now is the various ways God's Spirit gets worked into our lives. This is complex and often misunderstood, but I want you to be informed and knowledgeable. Remember how you were when you didn't know God, led from one phony god to another, never knowing what you were doing, just doing it because everybody else did it? It's different in this life. God wants us to use our intelligence, to seek to understand as well as we can. For instance, by using your heads, you know perfectly well that the Spirit of God would never prompt anyone to say "Jesus be damned!" Nor would anyone be inclined to say "Jesus is Master!" without the insight of the Holy Spirit.

God's various gifts are handed out everywhere; but they all originate in God's Spirit. God's various ministries are carried out everywhere; but they all originate in God's Spirit. God's various expressions of power are in action everywhere; but God himself is behind it all. Each person is given something to do that shows who God is: Everyone gets in on it, everyone benefits. All kinds of things are handed out by the Spirit, and to all kinds of people! The variety is wonderful:

wise counsel
clear understanding
simple trust
healing the sick
miraculous acts
proclamation
distinguishing between spirits
tongues
interpretation of tongues.

All these gifts have a common origin, but are handed out one by one by the one Spirit of God. He decides who gets what, and when.

You can easily enough see how this kind of thing works by looking no further than your own body. Your body has many parts—limbs, organs, cells—but no matter how many parts you can name, you're still one body. It's exactly the same with Christ. By means of his one Spirit, we all said good-bye to our partial and piecemeal lives. We each used to independently call our own shots, but then we entered into a large and integrated life in which he has the final say in everything. (This is what we proclaimed in word and action when we were baptized.) Each of us is now a part of his resurrection body, refreshed and sustained at one fountain—his Spirit—where we all come to drink. The old labels we once used to identify ourselves—labels like Jew or Greek, slave or free—are no longer useful. We need something larger, more comprehensive.

I want you to think about how all this makes you more significant, not less. A body isn't just a single part blown up into something huge. It's all the different-but-similar parts arranged and functioning together. If Foot said, "I'm not elegant like Hand, embellished with rings; I guess I don't belong to this body," would that make it so? If Ear said, "I'm not beautiful like Eye, limpid and expressive; I don't deserve a place on the head," would you want to remove it from the body? If the body was all eye, how could it hear? If all ear, how could it smell? As it is, we see that God has carefully placed each part of the body right where he wanted it.

But I also want you to think about how this keeps your significance from getting blown up into self-importance. For no matter how significant you are, it is only because of what you are a part of. *An enormous eye or a gigantic hand wouldn't be a body, but a monster. What we have is one body with many parts, each its proper size and in its proper place. No part is important on its own. Can you imagine Eye telling Hand, "Get lost; I don't need you"? Or, Head telling Foot, "You're fired; your job has been phased out"? As a matter of fact, in practice it*

*works the other way—the "lower" the part, the more ba-
sic, and therefore necessary. You can live without an eye,
for instance, but not without a stomach. When it's a part
of your own body you are concerned with, it makes no difference whether the part is visible or clothed, higher or
lower. You give it dignity and honor just as it is, without
comparisons. If anything, you have more concern for the
lower parts than the higher. If you had to choose, wouldn't
you prefer good digestion to full-bodied hair?*

*The way God designed our bodies is a model for un-
derstanding our lives together as a church: every part
dependent on every other part, the parts we mention and
the parts we don't, the parts we see and the parts we don't.
If one part hurts, every other part is involved in the hurt,
and in the healing. If one part flourishes, every other part
enters into the exuberance.*

*You are Christ's body—that's who you are! You must
never forget this. Only as you accept your part of that
body does your "part" mean anything. You're familiar
with some of the parts that God has formed in his church,
which is his "body":*

apostles
prophets
teachers
miracle workers
healers
helpers
organizers
those who pray in tongues.

*But it's obvious by now, isn't it, that Christ's church
is a complete Body and not a gigantic, unidimensional
Part? It's not all Apostle, not all Prophet, not all Miracle
Worker, not all Healer, not all Prayer in Tongues, not all
Interpreter of Tongues. And yet some of you keep compet-
ing for so-called "important" parts.*

But now I want to lay out a far better way for you.
—Paul, writing in 1 Corinthians 12, MSG
(emphasis in original)

This chapter of Paul's letter to the Corinthians leads into his famous chapter describing love. Love is the better way. Love is the heart of God. Love is the essential component of the image of God that defines Him, transforms us, and will one day define us as well.

Everything comes back to God. The Kingdom of God, the Kingdom of Heaven, the Body of Christ, the Church, Christianity, the Mission, the Mission Field, evangelism, discipleship, the Exodus, life, resurrection, calling, purpose, meaning, humanity... it all has a beginning and an end: God. The Bible says that God is the Alpha and the Omega, which is a reference to the Greek alphabet where Alpha is the first letter and Omega is the last letter (Revelation 22:13). It is a statement meaning that God is the beginning and the end. He is the source and the purpose. He is the start and the finish. It comes from Him and goes towards Him. This isn't simply some matter of poetry or metaphorical philosophy inspired to call people to think of how huge God is. This is actually the fact of the matter: God is the beginning and He is the end.

I believe that the Gospel has been severely wounded and corrupted in our North American situation. We've fallen into the familiar trap of history, and replaced God with man. Because of this, we've missed where we come from, and, tragically, where we were meant to go. So often people have seen an issue with the world and tried to fix it, only to later discover that their remedy was just a new form of the same evil. The only way anything can ever change for good is to return it to God. It must be brought back to its origin, its source, its creator. We must be remade into the colourful snapshots of God that we were meant to be.

I believe that even within the realm of perfect creation before the fall of man, before we ruined everything, creation had the same purpose as it does now. God isn't simply the end goal because we have strayed from Him.

God has always been the focus and goal.

God has always been the purpose.

To reflect His image has always been the point. In the garden of Eden, humanity and all of creation were designed to display the glory, love, care, creativity, and justice of God. Now, we are on the journey of being restored to that same condition.

Everything we do is to come from God and have Him as the end goal and purpose. If we work to spread the Word of God, we do so only by the power of God so that other people will come to Him and be restored to His image. When we go to work at a soup kitchen, we are seeking to love people as Christ has loved us, by His victory over sin and selfishness, so that others may know His love and so our community may reflect the image of God. I need to deal with the sin and baggage in my life so that I can better reflect His image in my life, so that others may see Him, so others may know Him, so others may be changed and restored to His image, so our world may glorify Him. But this only comes from His power, His work, His Holy Spirit. It only comes through Jesus returning His image to us. Without Him we cannot be the Image. It all begins with Him, and has its end in Him.

This may seem redundant, or overly repetitive, but it is a necessary concept to grasp if we are to be the exploding kingdom. In the previous chapter we discussed how we need to bless others and not ourselves; we need to explode rather than implode. We need to stop asking, "what can I get away with?" and start asking, "what is beneficial for others, and honouring to God?" Like what Paul mentions in 1 Corinthians 10:23, saying that even though everything is permissible, not everything is beneficial.

We must remember that it is God who determines what is beneficial and what isn't. It is God who provides the power and ability to move towards what is beneficial. God Himself is the source of the beneficial. It is holiness, Christ-likeness, that is beneficial—not our wills or our power. It isn't our resources or

our insights that make a difference or add value to this world—
it's God.

When we look at the problems of the world—hunger, obesity, illness, corruption, poverty, tragedy, loss—we must remember that it isn't us who fixes these things, and it isn't money that
changes things or solves problems. The only solution is God.
When we are His image, things change. When He changes us to
reflect Him, things change. When we give up our will, our demands, and allow Him to dictate who we are, things change.

Money won't change the world, but obedience will.

People have been throwing money at problems for years and
years, and those problems still exist. Poverty isn't solved by giving money to people. Hunger isn't simply solved by the richest
people in the world giving all their money to feed the hungry.
Would that help? Yes... for a time, until the money ran out, unless
the people used the resources to get out of their cycles of poverty.
But most won't. People don't change just because someone gives
them money. People aren't made happy just because they have
money. Just read the news: every month or so there is a new story
about some sports star or celebrity, with more money than I can
properly imagine, that has taken their own life or done something
stupid and ended up in prison. Their money and resources didn't
change their lives.

Our efforts won't change our lives or the lives of others. This
is one of the key reasons why God commanded the Israelites to
honour the Sabbath, to keep it holy, and to not work on that day.
When we honour the Sabbath by not working, we have to depend
on God to sustain and provide, because we aren't doing anything
to sustain ourselves. We have to trust Him to provide, to work,
and to change. He is the power that changes things. It has to start
with God, and move towards Him.

In order to begin with God, we have to know Him. Again, this
may seem redundant or overly obvious, but it's absolutely vital
that we acknowledge and focus on this fact. In order to change
our world, to explode, to love others the way Christ loves them

and loves us, we need to know how Christ would have us love them. Some of this is simple and clear. Some of this comes from a sincere study of His Word. But much of it comes from an ongoing conversation with Him. We have to know God, know His voice, and speak with Him in order to know what to do, when to do it, and how to do it.

It is similar to any working relationship. The more we know who we are working with, the more we understand what they mean when they say certain things and what they want done. Sometimes we need to have special meetings to figure out all the ins and outs of a situation. Sometimes we need to just take directives without knowing why because there is too much going on for us to try to wrap our heads around it all, or because we aren't ready to know what else is happening. Sometimes we immediately know what needs to happen because we have seen how our boss or partner works in these situations. Then, other times, we need to wait for a signal from them as to what the next delicate move should be.

We have to know God and be listening to Him all the time. Obedience is the key. It won't be money, time, effort, blood, sweat, or tears that change hearts and change our world—only obedience to God. It has to come from Him. We cannot fabricate the image of God.

This relationship with God that changes us, guides us, and leads us begins with worship. Worship is the vertical aspect of the image. It's where God sends love to us and we reciprocate it back to Him. We don't have love to give Him without Him first giving it to us, since He is the creator and source of love. To try to give love without God is like trying to breathe without air.

He loves us first, then we give it back to Him, then He sends more love, and we give it back to Him again; this is worship. This goes on and on, and the love He gives us begins to overflow from us because it's too much for us to contain and it spills out onto others, which creates the horizontal aspect of the image. As we begin to love God and others properly, the image is manifested in us and people around us begin to experience God. But it starts with worship. It's worship that honours God as One, as Worthy, as Holy. It's worship that submits to and acknowledges God as first and last. It's worship that glorifies Him in the highest.

He is the goal. Our mission is God—by God, for God. We are to be His image on Earth. The church is the Body of Christ. Christ is God made flesh, made human, the true image of God manifested in human form, what we *were* supposed to look like. What we *are* supposed to look like.

Just as the diagrams in Chapter Five show, we are to love God and others, just as the Father loves the Son and the Spirit.

It is about explosive living. *Agape*. God.

Our mission is to be the image of God. When we are the image of God, we reflect God to the world and give Him glory. When we are the image of God, we are human and are being perfected and sanctified until the day *we* are glorified. By being the image, we bring Him honour, we become who we were designed to be, and we reach out in ways that bring others to the image as well.

God humbled Himself to come to us; we must humble ourselves to go to others.

God suffered to provide for us; we must suffer to provide for others.

God loved us even when we were hypocrites; we need to love people even when they are hypocrites.

God was patient when people in the family were being stupid; we need to be patient with people in our families (biological or social) when they are being stupid.

God went out of His way to heal people's bodies; we need to care for our bodies and work to heal and restore those of other people.

God fed the hungry; we need to feed the hungry.

God got rid of the garbage of His people's culture; we need to get rid of the garbage in our culture.

God focused on the best social and familial dynamics that would create the environment and society that worked according to His design; we need to conform to His designs and see that they work.

God condemned sin because it destroys people and relationships; we need to condemn sin because it destroys life and the image of God.

God fought for others and not Himself; we need to fight for others and not ourselves.

Jesus walked our path so we could walk His. He gave us the power to be human.

I could go on, but essentially, it comes down to holiness, which is Christ-likeness, or being the image of God. Getting people "saved" isn't our mission. Helping people become the image of God is—and, consequently, that *is* salvation. We aren't saved to heaven—we are saved to holiness. Christianity isn't about checking boxes and going to heaven—it's about being restored to the Image of God. And we cannot properly be the Image alone. We are the Church; we are the body; *we* are the Image. This is how we bring glory to God, and this is how we become truly human.

See, we are only human when we reflect God.

This is the only way to bring Him honour.

He is the beginning, and the end.

He is our mission.

The crazy thing about all this is that when we get into the thick of it, it doesn't seem like work. It just fits. It flows like we were meant for it. There is so much fulfillment and joy in this giving, sacrifice, surrender, submission, suffering, and obedience that it sometimes leaves us wondering who is being blessed more—ourselves or the people we are serving.

This personal meaning and blessing cannot be the motive, but it is a result of the change Christ makes in us. We end up wanting more and more and more of His image to overwhelm us. We seek with greater and greater passion to know Him, to glorify Him, to love Him. He becomes our growing passion, and we seek this because we want to love *Him* more, because we want to love *others* more, and we recede into the background because we know the value of the treasure we have found in this field.

If you get this, there is an old hymn that may sum up the cry of your heart: "Oh to Be Like Thee" by Thomas O. Chisholm.

Oh! to be like Thee, blessed Redeemer,
This is my constant longing and prayer;
Gladly I'll forfeit all of earth's treasures,
Jesus, Thy perfect likeness to wear.

Refrain:
Oh! to be like Thee, oh! to be like Thee,
Blessed Redeemer, pure as Thou art;
Come in Thy sweetness, come in Thy fullness;
Stamp Thine own image deep on my heart.

Oh! to be like Thee, full of compassion,
Loving, forgiving, tender and kind,
Helping the helpless, cheering the fainting,
Seeking the wand'ring sinner to find.

Oh! to be like Thee, lowly in spirit,
Holy and harmless, patient and brave;
Meekly enduring cruel reproaches,
Willing to suffer, others to save.

Oh! to be like Thee, Lord, I am coming,
Now to receive th' anointing divine;
All that I am and have I am bringing,
Lord, from this moment all shall be Thine.

Oh! to be like Thee, while I am pleading,
Pour out Thy Spirit, fill with Thy love,
Make me a temple meet for Thy dwelling,
Fit me for life and Heaven above.[14]

This is the point of Christianity, the point of the Gospel. It's about us, but it isn't. It's about the Way of Jesus. In the book of Acts when the Church first began, people started making fun of those who followed Christ by calling them "Christ-ians." But these Christians didn't call their belief system Christianity, they called it the Way.

It wasn't about a set of beliefs and ideas; it was about a way of life. It was about the way that Jesus lived. It was about the Way of Jesus. Christians were originally called "followers of the Way." The Way is to be like Jesus. And who is Jesus but the manifested second person of the Trinity in humanity?

To be like Jesus. To be like God in the flesh... but not to be God, for Jesus made it quite clear in how He modeled life that even though He was God, He didn't hold His equality up for all to see and instead submitted Himself, giving us the example that as humans, not God, we too must submit and not attempt to be God. We are to live like He would if He were a human.

God is the origin, He is the Way, and He is the goal. We become truly human by His power, so we can look like Jesus and be like Him, free from sin and the power of death, so we can show and share the image of God. When we live like Christ, things change—we change.

When the Holy Spirit comes and fills us, we become who we were created to be. Our baggage begins to be dealt with, and doesn't hold us down anymore. Our habits begin to change, and our motives get straightened out so that our default desires are purified. Our natural reactions begin to stem from this new heart we have, and we begin to form habits that are naturally honouring to God. Our relationships begin to change, and we begin to fight for others. Healing takes place in the deep dark corners of our souls, and we find a liberating confidence in an identity based on the Word of God. Our weaknesses don't matter anymore, because they are just areas where God can show how He is able to take what is broken and still use it for His purpose. We begin to run towards God, towards holiness, towards the heavenly design of reality, away from the selfish and hellish way of things, and though there is much conflict and confrontation, things just start to work better.

Then as we grow closer to God, and know Him better, we find that we know ourselves better, and others better. He is the beginning and the end.

Start in the right place, and don't misplace the ending.

CHAPTER FOURTEEN

HOLISTIC GOSPEL

Though I've attempted to make it clear how this message is more than just intellectual and idealistic, there remains an enormous risk that those who have read this book, or portions of it, will simply nod their heads in agreement or shake their heads in disagreement, and never actually take it to mean what it really means. There is an incredible risk that this message will remain just another stale idea that those who are religious will grasp and hold onto, studying and examining, all the while never living it. There's nothing more ironic than this, yet it remains a significant possibility.

There also remains the risk that someone will attempt to take something out of context. And there is the reality that I've most likely missed something vital that should have been expressed. Yet I can't worry about these things. I think I've done all I can to be faithful in this process, and I believe that God is both big enough to fill in the gaps as well as gracious enough to be working on people from more than one angle. He is living and active, so the fact that I've missed things or made mistakes isn't the end of the world.

But what if we know about the image of God and still don't live it out?

God has said that if we refuse to praise Him, He will make the rocks cry out in worship (Luke 19:40). Unfortunately, I believe this has already happened. Not to be funny—please excuse the pun, but I've seen more worship at a rock concert than I have seen in some churches. In all seriousness, I've left the concert of a secular rock band and felt more in tune with God than while sitting in some church services. I've watched the relativistic and very religiously confused Oprah live out more Christ-like love at times than many devoted church goers. I've seen governments, atheists, secular organizations, and people who hate Christianity show more concern for justice, health, poverty, hunger, slavery, and the wellbeing of people and the world than many, if not most, churches.

I think God will be glorified one way or another, and I think because many of us "Christians" aren't willing to live in a way that gives Him glory, He is using the rocks. He is using people with wrong motives and dark hearts to do good in spite of themselves... because we haven't.

This isn't just a theology that is centered around a mental ascent or intellectual academic pursuit. This is about life and being. It is about our lives. It's about how we talk, how we sleep, how we walk and work and think and brush our teeth. It's about how we work as a community: our goals, our ambitions, our finances, our time, our relationships, our furniture, our cars, our clothes, our ideas, our businesses, our environments. It's about the poor here, and the starving around the world. It's about those enslaved to poverty and abuse, and those who are trapped in sin and addiction. It's about how we spend our money, who we look at, what we do, and what we don't do. It's about who we really are.

I'm not saying that we become something according to what we do, but rather that who we are shows through what we do. We sometimes forget it, or try to ignore it, but I think deep down we all know it. It's even explicit in movies. If you've seen *Batman*

Begins it's right there throughout the film (seriously, it's a repeated piece of dialogue).[15]

If it produces apples, it's an apple tree. If it produces blueberries, it's a blueberry bush. If we produce actions of selfishness, we are selfish, and if we produce actions of *agape*, we are like Christ. It's what's on the inside that comes out. Jesus said, *"...the mouth speaks what the heart is full of"* (Luke 6:45, NIV). If we claim to be Christians and don't look like Christ, and aren't being changed to look like Him, we aren't Christians.

We cannot have the image of God, the life of Christ, the change and power of the Holy Spirit, and still act the same as we used to. We cannot be alive in Christ intellectually and dead in our actions. We cannot have salvation and not be living and growing in the image of God, for being remade in the image of God *is* salvation. It's a salvation that begins now and spreads into eternity and incorruption. Yet, so many will believe they can know and love God while not being conformed to His image—and the rocks will cry out.

Again, I'm not saying we earn salvation, or that if we don't perform perfectly we lose our salvation. I don't think what we have done, or even where we are right now, is as important to God as the direction we are headed. If we're messing up but moving in the right direction, growing in Him and seeking Him and falling along the way, that's called growth. However, if we are set in our ways, aren't seeking Him or working on change, and maybe even actively looking away from Him, we have to admit that we might be in trouble!

It's time for us to claim what is stated in 1 Peter. It's time that we accepted our call to be who Peter says we are:

But you are a chosen people, a royal priesthood, a holy nation, God's special possession, that you may declare the praises of him who called you out of darkness into his wonderful light. Once you were not a people, but now you

are the people of God; once you had not received mercy,
but now you have received mercy.

—1 Peter 2:9–10, NIV

Holy. Royal. Nation. Priesthood. Not just in one area and idea of life, but in everything. This Gospel was never meant to be segregated. This Gospel was always intended to affect everything. It is the solution. It is the only solution. It is the only Way.

Consider the poverty problem in the world. Poverty is found in inner city regions and rural settings in North America, entire communities in South America, countries in Africa, certain castes in Asia, and all around the world. It's built on cultural and sociological cycles. In the U.S. many occurrences of poverty come from a lack of education. Some areas are cheap to live in, but have few honest job opportunities, which means the schools are terrible. Students then have fewer opportunities to grow and get better jobs, end up in trouble, and do what everyone else does. Then they have kids and the cycle begins again. Until they have better schools, things won't change. But then, even schools won't fix it.

We need to break the mentality that says "You need to just survive until tomorrow by any means necessary." We need to break the cycle of mistrust and change the culture. We need to get rid of the greed of those who lord it over them, and we need to get rid of the fear in those who are caught in it. I know of no other solution to these things than by the fulfilling of the image of God in the lives and relationships of those who are caught in these cycles.

If we lived the Gospel, we wouldn't attempt to keep all the funding in our area for our schools, but would be forcing it into the areas that need it most. We wouldn't be spending our time on the golf course for our own entertainment, but teaching skills to those who've never had the opportunity, fixing up broken houses and communities. Hope would be shared, and those who were caught in cycles of mistrust, broken families, drugs, addiction, etc. would be freed from those bonds and able to begin thinking long term, considering what is best for a future beyond today. There would be no shortage of food or funds for those that need help breaking cycles, and there would be no shortage of desire to break the cycles. It wouldn't be about deserving handouts; it would be about becoming all that God intended us to be, with everyone helping everyone else move forward. The rich helping the poor, and the poor teaching the rich.

It wouldn't be just about throwing money at a problem, it would be about fixing the problem.

If we care about our bodies because they are the temple of the Holy Spirit, and we are the image of God, we must take care of them (1 Corinthians 6:19). From healthy eating, exercising, developing good habits, and taking care of our teeth, we need to care for our bodies. Consider that the reduction of plaque on teeth reduces health risks to our hearts. The care of our teeth helps ensure self-confidence so we aren't afraid to smile, and enables us to eat the food we need to be healthy, which opens doors, creates opportunities, and helps us be more productive for longer, all the while enjoying this life God has provided.

Consider what happens when we avoid gluttony, start to exercise, and make sure that we are healthy, not obese or too small. This gives us more energy, enabling us to enjoy life as well as to contribute to the lives of others. We avoid a plethora of health problems, reduce health care costs, and free up more funds for those in need. We also avoid eating food that is bad for us, returning us to good and natural foods that come from farms and home gardens. We then support local economies, and also encourage positive treatment of foreign markets and regions, such as in South America with the production of bananas and coffee beans, thus enabling others to make an appropriate living from their work.

If we love others as Christ has loved us (John 15:12), because it isn't good to be alone (Genesis 2:18), and because we are meant to be the image of God, we begin working to bless others and not to amass personal wealth. Our priority becomes the welfare of those around us, not our own wallets or bellies. Think about what would happen if in our businesses we started to fight for our employees and their families, even if it meant we would take a pay cut. An environment would be created where means of education, health care, and community events for employees would be provided so they could grow more and more healthy, and so they in turn would be able to bless others. We would seek to help those who are stuck in ruts and are unable to break cycles on their own by giving them opportunities to change and grow.

Risking our success and money because people are more important than those things would result in the loss of the gap between the rich and the poor, because those with money would use it to help those without it. But, again, this isn't just about giving handouts, it's about giving love, community, listening ears, counsel, investment, education, hope, purpose, and jobs. If we did this we would find ourselves in a community where people would look to their neighbours and actively try to include and love them so no one would be left out.

When we apply the image of God to our lives and our relationships, it becomes apparent that marriage is something worth valuing and fighting for, not just for legal and moral reasons, but because it is the foundation for building a healthy society, raising children, and creating a legacy that is both useful and not easily shaken. A relationship between a man and a woman, not just for personal gain, or until personal desire wanes, but built on the commitment that two different yet complementary persons united with God will stay with each other and work through every problem and every situation regardless of personal cost, fear, or time, is one that reflects the image of God and builds healthy community. When this happens, kids grow up in one home without being abandoned or fought over by their parents. Diversity and unity are expressed, and they begin to see how conflict isn't the end, but just a part of growing together. This lays the foundation for all healthy relationships and helps to build personal character. If children grew up with both parents, we would see our prisons reduced to half, psychologists and psychiatrists having to look for work, much of the debt crisis remedied, poverty reduced, and schools focused on teaching, not babysitting.

In this Gospel, we find out who we were meant to be, that God created us in His image (Genesis 1:27), and that Christ came to restore us, freeing us from the dominion and slavery of selfishness, anger, depression, sin, and the fear of death. We begin to see opportunities rather than problems. Even the idea of death doesn't hold us back, because it isn't the end. We're able to enjoy life and give enjoyment to others because we aren't crippled by fear. Cycles of anger and depression are conquered so we can actually accept help from others and grow beyond where we have been stuck.

At the same time, success is redefined so that it isn't based on what others think or do, but on who God is and who He has made us to be. We stop trying to be someone else, and we embrace the purpose God has placed in and on us. We are content to be who we are and we realize we are fighting beside each other, not against each other. Loneliness, self-entitlement and fear shrivel up and die.

This Gospel of the Image of God reveals the plot, or intended storyline, of our lives:

We take care of our resources so we can make the greatest impact on those around us.

We pay our taxes honourably so we can support our community.

We eat food that is good for us and provide food for our families and many others.

We care for our bodies because Jesus healed people physically, meaning that the physical is obviously important to God.

We feed the hungry.

We fight obesity.

We give up anything that gets in the way so we can help others deal with their addictions.

We pick up garbage in order to protect the environment, which is the world God created and we messed up.

We take a stand against slavery because no one should be abused.

We fight for marriages between one man and one woman because family is the essential building block of a society that is functional and sustainable and is the pattern God originally intended for us.

We stand against sexual obsession, addiction, slavery, abuse, and consumerism, because sex and intimacy are sacred.

We run our businesses to provide for people, giving them the best while serving those who serve us, creating a mutually beneficial relationship.

We stop supporting politics that require dishonesty and greed so that the corruption can be reduced and funds can actually be used appropriately. (We should examine our own government, as well as the reasons why foreign aid to many countries is ineffective. Typically, the funds never make it to the people.)

We invest in people more than technology, because it isn't just about money.

The Gospel affects our:
Marriages
Diet
Habits
Spending
Thoughts
Ideas
Emotions
Ways of parenting
Rights
College atmospheres
Philosophies
Science
Corporate policies

Educational systems
Politics
Use of drugs and alcohol
Etc.

If we name anything, we can find a way that the Gospel affects it. Even something as weird as insulating our homes is connected with the Gospel. We should insulate our homes, because it will save money in the long run, which enables us to use our funds more appropriately to serve others and sustain our family's needs better and for longer.

And on the subject of money, using credit and building up a kingdom of things while incurring debt is both unfulfilling and unwise. The Gospel of the image of God would have us get rid of our unnecessary things, work to free us of debt, build the discipline to become a good steward of our resources, and then fight for others, not lay the burden on someone else so we can have worthless and fleeting entertainments.

The Gospel is holistic. It affects everything, and in turn changes everything about our world.

This leads us to the question that really matters: What are we going to do now? Yes, there are other questions like, "What does all this really mean to me?" and "How do we apply what we have just read?" and "How can we actually make a difference?" But in reality, these questions are only secondary. They are the ideas, not the actual actions. When it comes right down to it—to this Gospel of the image of God, to the Gospel of Christ—we are faced with an opportunity and a question: "What are we going to do now?"

Let's be blunt. As I write the first draft of this book, I'm not an old man, I'm only twenty-five. I haven't written this book because I want to be famous, or because I think I am smarter than anyone else. I am actually surprised at how many pages I've used to say so little.

I've written this book because I'm tired.

I'm tired of sitting around watching people die and go to hell. I'm tired of watching people live through hell on earth, children starving, men abandoning their families, women living for lust rather than love, families being torn apart, society imploding as individuals fight for the right to do what they want rather than what is best. Tired of social movements that carry the air of being righteous and pure when they only create havoc and will result in the confusion and degradation of more lives. Tired of sex being the thing everything has to do with. Tired of food, a substance designed to sustain life, being served and consumed in a way that actually steals life and causes despair, depression, immobility, hate, greed, and oppression. I'm tired of history repeating itself, where once Africans were enslaved so we could have sugar, and now the entire world is enslaved so we can have banks and investments and armies and governments that are more focused on themselves than the people they "serve." I'm tired of Christianity doing more harm than good, spreading some kind of perverted and corrupted flimsy Gospel.

I'm tired of the rest of the world having more concern for the wellbeing of people than the Church does. I'm tired of people wanting to do something to change the world, and putting their effort into things that are either useless, fruitless, or blind because no one has been able to explain to them what the real problems and solutions are. To be honest, I'm tired of this tiny and sick definition of love that says, "The only way to love people is to give them the right to do whatever they want." I'm so tired of both the Church and the world believing that.

I'm tired of going to a rock show and seeing more *agape* love shared from the stage than from a group of Christians. I'm tired of killing babies and avoiding old people because we're afraid they will somehow diminish our lives, as if the addition and maintenance of an actual living being takes away from life.

I'm tired of weighing the costs of saving the world in an attempt to make it affordable.

I'm tired of looking at the Church and their flimsy gospel that just leaves people stuck in their sin, waiting to die, making no difference in their lives and no difference in the world around them. I'm tired of the Church giving the world ammunition to run the name of Jesus through the mud because we are a bunch of hypocrites who claim to know God but proclaim a message that is so pathetic and limited that we continue to gorge ourselves on sin and become proficient in lying to ourselves about how the sins in our lives aren't really sins. I'm tired of letting the enemy, the deceiver, win. I'm tired of a flimsy gospel that is so powerless that it can be proclaimed to millions of people without offending or moving them.

I'm tired of people being lost in their own skin and so afraid of those around them that loneliness has stepped in and sucked their souls dry.

I'm tired of people being enslaved to money, wealth, and materialism, making them anxious and worried, always striving and never achieving. I'm tired of them avoiding the simple life and being rewarded by ulcers and stress.

I'm tired of humanism.

I'm tired of people trying to find what they are allowed to do, rather than what they need to do.

I'm tired of shallow beliefs.

I'm tired of giving the world reasons to hate Christians because we are selfish, rather than giving them reasons to hate us because we actually follow Christ, which takes power away from them.

I'm tired of trying to fix the world by my power.

I'm tired of being sinful.

I'm tired.

We have been given everything we need to be godly (2 Peter 1:3). This is the Gospel. And even though the love and work of God is unconditional, relationship isn't. We have a choice. He gives us what we need; will we choose to submit, or to stand against Him in defiance? Will we embrace the image of God, die to our own wills and be born again, fresh and remade, to be like Christ?

Or will we continue to rebel, killing ourselves and destroying the world and the people God created?

Will we live with a flimsy Gospel, or with a powerful Gospel from a powerful God?

Will we be intentional and consistent?

Will we forget who God is—and consequently forget who we are—or will we remember the Exodus?

In the book of James, the author says this:

> *But don't just listen to God's word. You must do what it says. Otherwise, you are only fooling yourselves. For if you listen to the word and don't obey, it is like glancing at your face in a mirror. You see yourself, walk away, and forget what you look like. But if you look carefully into the perfect law that sets you free, and if you do what it says and don't forget what you heard, then God will bless you for doing it.*
> —James 1:22–25, NLT

Now that you have stared into the image of God, and looked intently at your own face, will you walk away and forget who you are—or will you remember? Will you become? Will you live out His image?

> *For now we see in a mirror dimly, but then face to face. Now I know in part; then I shall know fully, even as I have been fully known.*
> —1 Corinthians 13:12, ESV

The whole purpose of God in redemption is to make us holy and to restore us to the image of God. To accomplish this He disengages us from earthly ambitions and draws us away from the cheap and unworthy prizes that worldly men set their hearts upon.

—A.W. Tozer[16]

REFERENCES

SCRIPTURE REFERENCES

Beginning
1 John 4:21 (MSG)
2 Corinthians 3:18 (NIV)

Chapter 1
Exodus 3:14 (NIV)
Exodus 14:14 (NLT)
Exodus 14:14 (MSG)
Genesis 1:1 (NIV)

Chapter 2
John 14:5–10 (ESV)
John 8:31–38 (ESV)

Chapter 3
Jeremiah 3:19 (NIV)
Jeremiah 20
Jeremiah 18:5–10
Jeremiah 18:8 (NIV)
John 17:3 (NIV)

Chapter 4
Matthew 3:15–17
Matthew 28:19 (NIV)
1 John 4:16 (NIV)
Luke 15:11–32
Daniel 3
John 1:1–14 (ESV)
Philippians 2:7–8 (MSG)
Matthew 4:1–11
John 11:46–50
John 16:7 (NIV)
Matthew 5:16

Chapter 5
Genesis 1:27 (ESV)
Genesis 2:18 (ESV)
Ephesians 4:22-24 (NIV)
Ephesians 5:1-2 (ESV)
Colossians 3:9-10 (NIV)
2 Corinthians 3:18 (NIV)
1 John 2:6 (NIV)
1 John 4:21 (MSG)
Genesis 1:28
Matthew 22:36–40
Genesis 2:18–25
Isaiah 58
1 John 4:20
Hosea 6:6
1 Corinthians 12
John 14
John 14:26
Acts 2:17
Acts 2:38
Romans 5:5
Romans 8:26
Hebrews 12:1–2

Chapter 6
"If" statements:
Exodus 19:5
Exodus 23:22
Deuteronomy 11
Jeremiah 22:4–5
Zechariah 6:15
John 8:31
John 13:17
John 15:5–10
Romans 8:17

Romans 13:4
Colossians 1:23
1 Peter 2:9 (ESV)

Chapter 7
Matthew 22:37–40 (ESV)
Deuteronomy 6:5 (NIV)
Deuteronomy 5:7–21 (NIV)
Leviticus 19:18 (ESV)
Leviticus 19:33–34 (ESV)
Leviticus 25:35–36 (ESV)
Ezekiel 34:1–6 (MSG)
Isaiah 58:1–9 (MSG)
Micah 6:8 (MSG)
Micah 3:1–7 (MSG)
Malachi 4:5
John 14:6 (NIV)
Matthew 22:37–40
John 3

Chapter 8
Genesis 2:18 (NIV)
1 Corinthians 11:12
Genesis 3:15 (ESV)
Genesis 12:1–3 (ESV)
Genesis 50:19–20 (ESV)
2 Samuel 11
John 11:46–50
Romans 8:28 (NIV)
1 Corinthians 15:55–57 (NIV)

Chapter 9
Ephesians 4:15 (NIV)
John 16:7 (ESV)
John 14:26 (ESV)

John 14:12, 16–17 (ESV)
Matthew 18:20 (ESV)
Matthew 5:16 (ESV)
1 Peter 2:12 (ESV)
Zechariah 8:23 (ESV)
Ephesians 5:1–2 (ESV)
Colossians 3:9–10 (ESV)

Chapter 10
John 3:1–21 (MSG)
Matthew 6:24 (NIV)
Romans 3:23
Hebrews 11:1 (NIV)
Mark 4:31–32
1 Corinthians 12:31 (MSG)
1 Corinthians 13
1 John 4:16
John 17:3

Chapter 11
Exodus 32
Exodus 17
Numbers 14
Deuteronomy 6:4–12, 20–21 (ESV)
Exodus 14:14 (NLT)
Deuteronomy 5:15 (NIV)
2 Samuel 7:23 (NIV)
Deuteronomy 15:15, 24:18
Joshua 9:9, 24:17
Judges 2:12, 6:8
1 Samuel 2:27, 10:18
1 Kings 8:53
Psalm 81:10
Psalm 106:21
Jeremiah 11:4

Daniel 9:15
Hosea 13:4
Joshua 5:10
2 Kings 23:21
2 Chronicles 30:1
Ezra 6:19
Revelation 12:11 (ESV)
2 Corinthians 1:3–4 (ESV)
2 Corinthians 5:14–21 (NIV)
Luke 22–23
John 1:29 (NIV)
1 Corinthians 5:7
Hebrews 2:14–18

Chapter 12
Ezekiel 34:1–6 (MSG)
Matthew 13:44
Matthew 13:45–46
Matthew 13:31-33
Romans 9:3 (ESV)
Romans 9:3 (MSG)
Matthew 6:10 (NIV)
Revelation 21:1–4 (NIV)

Chapter 13
1 Corinthians 12 (MSG)
Revelation 22:13
1 Corinthians 10:23

Chapter 14
Luke 19:40
Luke 6:45 (NIV)
1 Peter 2:9–10 (NIV)
1 Corinthians 6:19
John 15:12

Genesis 2:18

Genesis 1:27

2 Peter 1:3

James 1:22–25 (NLT)

1 Corinthians 13:12 (ESV)

CITATIONS

1 Peter Furler & Steve Taylor, "Lost the Plot," on *Take Me to Your Leader* by Newsboys (Star Song Communications/Capitol CMG Publishing, 1996).

Chapter 1

2 James Strong, "Charash" H2790, in *The New Strong's Complete Dictionary of Bible Words* (Nashville, TN: Thomas Nelson Publishers, 1996), p. 337.

Chapter 2

3 L. Wachowski et al., *The Matrix* (Burbank, CA: Warner Home Video, 2001).

4 C. S. Lewis, *Till We Have Faces: A Myth Retold* (Toronto: A Harvest Book Harcourt, Inc., 1984), p. 294.

Chapter 3

5 A.W. Tozer, *The Pursuit of God/The Pursuit of Man Pocket Devotional* (Camp Hill: Christian Publications, Inc., 2002), p. 4.

6 James Strong, "Nacham" H5162, in *The New Strong's Complete Dictionary of Bible Words* (Nashville, TN: Thomas Nelson Publishers, 1996), p. 451.

Chapter 4

7 Quoted in Stephen Seamands, *Ministry in the Image of God: The Trinitarian Shape of Christian Service* (Downers Grove, Illinois: InterVarsity Press, 2009), p. 58.

Chapter 8

8 David Wilkerson, John & Elizabeth Sherrill, *The Cross and the Switchblade* (New York: Random House, 1963).

9 Howard Hendricks, teaching at Catalyst Conference in Atlanta (Recording Cat00ATL_-HowardHendricks_S8), 44 min.

Chapter 9

10 John Mayer, "Belief," on *Continuum* by John Mayer (Aware, Columbia Records, 2006).

Chapter 10

11 C.S. Lewis, *The Problem of Pain,* in *The Complete C.S. Lewis Signature Classics* (New York, NY: HarperCollins, 2002 [1940]), p. 626.

12 J.R.R. Tolkien, *The Two Towers: Being the Second Part of The Lord of the Rings* (Hammersmith, London: HarperCollins, 1994), pp. 414–415, 422–423.

Chapter 12

13 Steven Spielberg et al., *Schindler's List* (Universal City, CA: MCA Universal Home Video, 1994).

Chapter 13

14 Thomas Chisholm, "Oh to Be Like Thee" (1897), public domain.

Chapter 14

15 Christopher Nolan et al., *Batman Begins* (Burbank, CA: Warner Home Video, 2005).

Ending

16 A.W. Tozer, *The Root of the Righteous* (Chicago: Moody Publishers, 2015), p. 31.

ABOUT THE AUTHOR

Evan Oxner began his career in full-time ministry almost ten years ago, but he has been in the church his entire life, growing up in Yarmouth, Nova Scotia. The call upon his life was evident to everyone around him as a child, but he only realized it personally the year before going to college. He attended Bethany Bible College (now Kingswood University) in Sussex, New Brunswick. He currently leads a growing church in Amherst, Nova Scotia, where he spends most of his time writing, speaking, and investing in leaders with the penetrating and simple truth of God's Word.

His wife Heidi ensures that life is exciting and worth living, while he makes sure they survive long enough to enjoy those moments! His raw honesty and intensity are balanced out by the beauty and lovability of his family.

Beyond his years in the church serving and being mentored, and his college degree, Evan has no special training or accomplishment that sets him apart from anyone else. He embraces this truth as a testimony to the power of God's Word. He really is just an ordinary guy embracing the extraordinary Word of God.

Contact Evan

Email: eoxner15@gmail.com

Facebook: fb.me/evanoxnerbooks or @evanoxnerbooks

Website: evanoxner.wordpress.com